AMERICA'S
MOM

 Perennial Currents
An Imprint of HarperCollins*Publishers*

AMERICA'S MOM

The Life, Lessons, and Legacy

— *of* —

ANN LANDERS

RICK KOGAN

A hardcover edition of this book was published in 2003 by William Morrow, an imprint of HarperCollins Publishers.

HarperCollins books may be purchased for educational, business, or sales promotional use. For information please write: Special Markets Department, HarperCollins Publishers Inc., 10 East 53rd Street, New York, NY 10022.

FIRST PERENNIAL CURRENTS EDITION PUBLISHED 2005.

Designed by Judith Abbate

The Library of Congress has catalogued the hardcover edition as follows:
Kogan, Rick.
    America's mom : the life, lessons, and legacy of Ann Landers / Rick Kogan.—1st ed.
        p. cm.
    ISBN 0-06-054478-3
        1. Landers, Ann.   2. Advice columnists—United States—Biography.
    I. Title.
PN4874.L23K64 2003
070'.92—dc21
[B]

                                                                    2003053992

ISBN 0-06-075098-7 (pbk.)

05   06   07   08   09   ❖/RRD   10   9   8   7   6   5   4   3   2   1

To my mom, Marilew

To Colleen and her mom, Anne

And, of course, to Eppie

Acknowledgments

The idea for this book was born in the days immediately following Eppie Lederer's death last year. Called upon to write a number of stories for the *Chicago Tribune* about my personal and professional relationship with the woman known to millions as Ann Landers, I began to receive phone calls from people across the country. Not only did they want to express their grief but also tell me how Ann Landers's column had affected, changed, and, in some cases they believed, saved their lives.

You callers are the ones who launched this project.

Principal among those who kept it afloat and on course are Colleen Sims, my wife, the brightest and most thoughtful person I know, who, pressed into editing duties, became, without overestimation, my collaborator; Sharon Barrett, an award-winning documentary film producer and my great friend for more than two decades, who proved herself the best researcher/

interviewer in America; and Kathy Mitchell and Marcy Sugar, whose enthusiasm, feedback, insights, and stories carried me through some dark days. My mother, Marilew, graciously took a trip back in time, with the aide of my brother, Mark, in order to provide essential details and observations. Rafe Sagalyn fought off those publishers interested only in "dirt" and led me to William Morrow and Jennifer Brehl, an editor whose patience, intelligence, and guidance made this book vastly better than it might have been, and her assistant, Kelly O'Connor, a bright young woman of great wit and infectuous good humor. At every twist and turn I found the folks at Morrow to be inspired professionals. Many I have yet to meet. To all I am indebted: attorney Chris Goff; Executive Vice President and Publisher Michael Morrison, Lisa Gallagher, VP, associate publisher, and director of marketing; Debbie Stier, senior director of publicity; Justin Loeber, director of publicity; Joyce Wong, the managing editor who oversaw the copyediting process, beautifully handled by Laurie McGee; copy chief Josh Frank; production manager Michael Conroy; cover designers Rich Aquan and Barbara Levine, and interior designer Judy Abbate.

On the home front, Ron Silverman, an immensely gifted editor, helped guide the first draft out of its doldrums, and Frank Pirruccello, a lawyer of uncommon good sense, became a good pal. My colleagues at the *Chicago Tribune Magazine*—helped in various ways, if only by quietly suffering my mood swings. Kelly McGrath and Kevin Bell of the Lincoln Park Zoo provided encouragement, feedback, and a great photo. My co-author (on *Everybody Pays*) and great pal, Maury Possley, was always there with an inspiring and helpful word.

A huge and ongoing debt to those who taught me about words and newspapering, primarily my father, Herman, M. W. Newman, Richard Christiansen, Gregory Favre, Henry Kisor, and Mike Royko. Thanks also to the hundreds of print and television reporters, writers, and interviewers whose previous articles and programs about Eppie allowed me to chart the course of her life and career in those years before I was born and when I was too young to notice. Of great value were three books previously written about Eppie: her daughter Margo Howard's *Eppie*; *Dear Ann, Dear Abby*, an unauthorized biography by Jan Pottker and Bob Speziale; and David Grossvogel's *Dear Ann Landers: Our Intimate and Changing Dialogue with America's Best-Loved Confidante.*

To all the people who shared personal stories about Eppie for this book—those that made it into print and those that didn't—thank you for sharing memories that were often very personal and sometimes painful. And, finally, thanks to Eppie, for living the life she lived.

AMERICA'S
MOM

Prologue

Dear Ann Landers:

Forgive the formality. But your being dead is not helping me here at all.

"Here" is in Elgin, Illinois, and I am standing in front of a warehouse-like building that houses Bunte Auction Services. Inside are about a million pieces of your life that once filled the apartment in which you lived on Lake Shore Drive in downtown Chicago, about thirty miles east of here and more than a few worlds apart.

The view from your place was great, a sweeping view north along the lakefront, full of sky and sun and sand. Even in the winters, it was something; waves helped by the wind and icy temperatures, freezing one on top of another and forming shapes from dreams and nightmares, as if some giant artist was creating an outdoor ice sculpture garden just for the eyes of those who could afford to live within such sumptuous views of Lake Michigan, whether they deserved to or not, appreciated it or not, saw it or not.

I know you did. You once said to me, staring out the window one winter night a couple of years before you died, "Doesn't it look like Picasso went crazy out there?" and I thought, Well, she does deserve to live here. She sees it.

But I could really use your help here now. The view in Elgin is artless, industrial. There are a few trees, bits of grass fringing faceless one-story buildings. And there's this woman talking to me about her husband. He died six days ago and she is saying, "We were married for thirty-eight years. If he were alive, he would be here. We had so much fun at auctions."

She is one of about two hundred people who have come here this November 23 Saturday in 2002, a little after noon. I haven't gone inside yet. I'm not ready. So here I am, trying to prepare myself to see some of your possessions, things you absolutely no longer need and maybe some you forgot you even had while you were alive. Yes, yes, yes, I am smoking, and I know how much you hated smoking, how much you wanted me (and everybody else on the planet) to stop. I thought that every time you wrote about the evils and sorrows of smoking in your column, which was often, you were sending personal messages to me. But, yes, I am smoking, and I'm telling you, for what it's worth, that I will really start thinking about quitting, once this day is over.

"What are you going to buy?" I ask this woman who is talking to me.

"I don't know. I just want to see how she lived," says the woman.

Is she going to be disappointed? Will what is inside tell her how you lived? Will it even give her a clue? I don't think that things define a life; they just make for more confusion. I'm sure of this because just a few weeks ago I was going through some of my old stuff. I found a picture of you with my father. It was taken in 1982. I don't know where it was taken, but I know you'll want to know this: You looked great. You always liked to look great, and that's why you didn't want anybody to see you while you were dying. You wanted people and friends and relatives to remember you as if from a pretty picture, smiling and dolled up, and not from a sad, final few days filled with real pain.

In the picture my father looks old. He was only sixty-eight. You were sixty-four. You were newspaper colleagues and pals for a long time and you wrote on the picture, "To Herman—my secret passion for 25 years." That was nice. He liked you.

I'm not sure why I kept this picture, but I first found it going through my father's papers after he died in 1988. My mother kept some things, my brother kept some, and I kept some. The things I kept are a few of his books and pictures, a black-and-white sport coat that is two sizes too big for me, and a tattered corduroy coat. I wear them both, and when I do, I feel good even though I look like a bum. The rest of my father's things we gave away. I don't believe much in keeping things that belonged to dead people. When someone dies, what I keep are memories, trusting that whatever stays through the years will be the important stuff.

I kept this picture of the two of you, though, and I can't remember why. That was a bad time for me. There was no burial, just quick cremation, and the memorial service didn't take place until six weeks after he died. You were there, I remember, and I think I scared you that day. I spoke last, after some of his friends, colleagues, his brother, and my brother. It was held at the Newberry Library, that brick, castlelike building on Chicago's Near North Side where scholars and writers come to research the lives of people and places long gone. It's across the street from a lovely little park known as Bughouse Square, where once lunatics, intellectuals, libertines, and any other jokers with agendas would get up on soapboxes and announce their causes, gripes, or philosophies.

Inside the Newberry I gave a talk that was, to many of you, shocking, an angry expression of disappointment that my dad had died of a heart attack after he said "See you later" to my mom and went off for a morning walk near their house in Michigan, and that that quick exit had prevented me from saying good-bye in a way that would have made me feel better.

I left the stage and walked over to a window as Billie Holiday's "God Bless the Child" blasted over the sound system. I was smoking then, too, but you didn't say a word about that when you came up, hugged me, and put a piece of paper in my hand.

"These are the two best psychiatrists I know. Call them and tell them I told you to call," you said.

"You think something's wrong?"

"Oh, yes," you said, dramatically. "Oh, yes."

I can't walk past the Newberry without thinking of that late

May afternoon in 1988. The combination of your concern—I never did call your psychiatrist pals—and the fact that most of my father's papers are now housed in some basement room at the library always makes me smile when I walk by the building and allows me to hear the faint but unmistakable sound of Billie Holiday, too.

But where was I? That's right, some of your papers are inside the Bunte building. There are a lot more in San Francisco, being auctioned off today and tomorrow at a place called Butterfield's. Are there any pictures inside of you and my dad? You and my mom? She was a friend for a while. Anything of you and me? We were friends, too.

But now, this woman is saying, "So you knew her?"

"Yes; I was her editor for the last five years."

"Well, that must have been interesting."

"It certainly was."

I have never been to an auction, so I don't know what to expect. I told myself, driving from the city, that I was coming here to meet people whose lives you changed, whose paths you altered. I don't expect to be buying anything, bidding on your papers or all the other things I think must be sitting inside. I am curious about what's in there. A chair that I sat in? A little dish once filled with candy? Anything that might remind me of you? Tell me something about you that I don't already know?

"The auction book says she had a lot of owls, Ann Landers, collected them, little statues of them, figurines, paintings of them," the woman is saying. "Do you think there will be owls inside? A lot of owls?"

"I'm not sure," I say. "Those owls were precious to her. So many of them came as gifts from people who were touched by her wisdom, her advice."

"Owls are nice," the woman says, and as she keeps talking I think that she is in the first stages in a long process of grieving (and/or healing) and wonder if there is not some word of comfort or advice I could give that might move her into an easier place than where she is now. And it occurs to me that this, in a less in-your-face fashion, is what you spent most of your life doing. How could it not drive you crazy?

A couple of days before the auction I was trying to calculate how many letters were mailed to you: 47 years, 7 days a week, 2,000 letters a day. I'm not good at math, but I can figure this out: 47 years times 365 days a year times 2,000 letters a day. That's 34,310,000 letters, give or take an adulterous husband or two.

Of course, you didn't read them all, couldn't have. But you read enough—the pains and problems, as well as a few joys and poems, of two generations of readers—that I will always wonder: How could it not drive you crazy?

You tried to tell me once, tried to explain. We were having dinner and were talking about your first and most influential editor, Larry Fanning, and we were amazed and pleased that, even though I was thirty-some years younger than you, I had known Larry and spent some time at his house when I was a kid. He and my father used to play tennis together, and sometimes I'd drive with my dad up from the city to these suburban tennis courts near where Larry lived, just to watch. And after they played we'd go over to Larry's house and I'd fool around in the yard and they would drink gin and tonics in their white tennis clothes.

"Larry was good fortune smiling on me," you told me. "I remember that during those first months when I was writing the column, I was overwhelmed by some of the letters I was getting. There was so much suffering, uncertainty. I told Larry and he said, 'Look, baby'—he always called me 'baby'—he said, 'Look baby, these things aren't happening to you. You've got to separate yourself from your readers.' That was crucial for me. Some of the letters are so sad. If I couldn't insulate myself, I'd have gone to pieces."

You never did go to pieces, not that I could tell, and now that I'm thinking about it, maybe all those letters kept you sane. You wrote something more than a quarter of a century ago that is very sane: "Since I began writing my column, I have learned plenty. I have learned how it is with the stumbling, tortured people in this world who have nobody to talk to. The fact that my column has been a success underscores for me, at least, the central tragedy of our society. The loneliness, the insecurity, the fear that bedevils, cripples, and paralyzes so many of us."

So what would you say to this woman talking to me about her dead husband?

All I can think of saying is, "Did you hear about Elvis's hair?"

And she says, "Huh?," and then she starts laughing as I tell her that just last Saturday somebody bought a small jar filled with Elvis Presley's hair. He, or maybe she—no one was willing to say—paid $115,000 for it. It was an auction that lasted twenty days, and there was a fierce last-minute bidding war at a place called MastroNet, Inc., in the Chicago suburb of Oak Brook.

Chicago, auction capital of the world! Elvis one week and you the next.

Elvis's hair was saved by someone named Homer "Gill" Gilleland, who cut the King's hair for more than twenty years. He supposedly saved Elvis's hair after every cut, gathering it together from where it had dropped onto the floor, bundling it in towels and keeping it in his house. After Elvis died in 1977, Gilleland started selling strands of the hair in a souvenir shop across the street from Presley's Memphis home, Graceland. Before Gilleland died in 1995, he gave a bag of the hair to a friend, who finally decided to sell it to provide some extra financial cushion for his retirement. In another auction, MastroNet sold a strand of John F. Kennedy's hair for about $3,000.

You would have gotten such a kick about what one person said in the papers about all this. John Reznikoff is a "celebrity hair expert." He lives in Westport, Connecticut. He works for a place called University Archives, a private company that sells memorabilia from historical figures. He claims to have hair from about a hundred celebrities: Marilyn Monroe, Einstein, Napoleon—"celebrities" like that.

"I'm happy that it went for a lot of money because it kind of confirms what I've been saying all along," Reznikoff told a reporter. "Hair collecting has really come into the twenty-first century."

Isn't that great? Maybe it's good you're no longer around, because I now remember something you said to a reporter, about ten years ago: "The world is moving so fast these days that I am running as fast as I can to keep up with the changes. It's exhausting, but exciting. I frankly admit, however, that I'm glad I have already lived the greater part of my life. I'm not sure I want to be around fifty years from now."

I'm ready to go inside now, I think. A TV crew has just pulled up, and a reporter and cameraman are going inside, and I'm holding the door for them. There will be other reporters here, and in San Francisco today and tomorrow, some of them scrounging for scandal.

That's part of this, too, part of what happens after a celebrity dies. You once said, "No one likes to think about dying, but occasionally we need to remember life's limitations." Now that you are dead, I have to think you finally, really do have all the answers. I'm here hoping that death is like a big sleep, maybe with the sound of a jazz quartet in the background, the way it would sound at 5 A.M. when everybody's gone home and the musicians are playing just for the fun of it. Is it different when you're famous and you're dead? Can you hear the questions coming from Earth? That, I imagine, could be very troublesome.

I started getting calls the day after you died, people wanting to know how you died. Not just what caused the death—everybody knew by then it was multiple myeloma, a blood cancer that attacks the bone marrow—but what your last days were like. Did she suffer? Was she in the hospital? At home? Who was there? I never returned those calls, and I didn't return the others: Who were her boyfriends? What does her twin sister, Dear Abby, have to say? What was she like to work with? What was she really like? How much did she love her job? Her daughter, Margo? Her grandchildren? What were her dark sides? What were her demons?

I should have told them about our cocaine night.

It happened a few days after the papers were filled with stories of then-presidential candidate George W. Bush refusing to say whether he had ever used the drug. You had been talking about this on the phone with Al Gore when I came to pick you up for dinner.

Later, sitting at a table in the International Club of the Drake Hotel, just down the block from your apartment, you asked, "Now, why won't Bush say whether he did it or not? And do you know anything about this drug?"

Having had some experience with life's shady sides and unsavory characters, I was able to tell you a bit. You then asked, "How exactly would a person use it?" I decided to demonstrate, as best I could, using salt from the shaker on the table and a dollar bill.

"Why the dollar bill?" you asked.

"Because I don't have a hundred," I said.

I leaned over and pretended to inhale the salt that I had spread in two neat little lines on the tablecloth. You noticed another couple staring at us.

"Do you think they know what we're pretending to do?" you asked.

"I can't imagine," I said.

"If they did, we'd be quite the scandal," you said, playfully.

"Good."

I handed you the tightly wound dollar bill—"Just a souvenir," I said—and you tucked it into the pocket of your stylish black jacket.

And now, here I am walking inside the auction house with this woman who thinks she's about to learn how you lived, and

I'm wondering if that rolled-up dollar could be part of the stuff inside. Maybe it's still tucked in the pocket of your jacket or sitting on its own: "Lot 1232B—DOLLAR BILL: With salt residue, used one evening by Ann Landers and unidentified companion, International Club, Drake Hotel."

I don't plan to bid on anything. But if that dollar bill is here, don't you think I should bid on that?

· LOT 1248W ·

Ann Landers 1936
Senior High School Yearbook

The yearbook is the Maroon & White. Central High School, Sioux City, Iowa. The year 1936 was not a good year in America, except perhaps for the hundreds of people staring from the pages of the book, faces mostly smiling, filled with the youthful hope and confidence and ignorance that would allow them to see the future beyond the Great Depression.

It always surprises people to learn that the person who would become Ann Landers was born and raised in Iowa. But Iowa was where Esther Pauline Friedman was born, if you're looking for all-American symbolism, on July 4, 1918. She came into the world seventeen minutes before her twin sister, who would be named Pauline Esther Friedman and who would become Abigail Van Buren, or Dear Abby, to most of those who have ever picked up a newspaper.

The Friedman family was big on nicknames, and almost immediately father Abraham, mother Rebecca, and the two older sisters, Dorothy and Helen, started referring to the babies as "Eppie" and "Popo," and that's how everyone would know them, into high school and far beyond. "My friends all call me Eppie," Eppie always said. "People who call me Ann are the people I don't know."

She also said, "I think I owe a lot to my Iowa heritage. I think that middle-American values have helped me tremendously— the principles, the morality. It was a place where neighbors cared about neighbors. And I mean really cared."

Eppie's yearbook is fascinating, a snapshot of an innocent time only older people can now remember, even down to the ads at the back of the book for the Sioux City Stock Yards, Richey's Barber Shop ("Neatness is one of the most important things in your life"), Blue Bunny Ice Cream ("Ask For It By Name"), Blue Barrel Soap ("Kind As a Kiss on Your Hands"), and Morey's ("Home of the Two-Pants Suit").

There are no ads for the theaters owned by Eppie and Popo's father. Abraham Friedman had come to America with his wife in 1908. They came, fleeing czarist pogroms and fearful that he might be conscripted into the army, from Vladivostok, Russia. They arrived in Sioux City speaking no English, having no money or any marketable skills. But Abe Friedman started buying chickens from farmers and peddling them to grocers from a horse-drawn cart. The horse was blind, so he was able to buy it for less than he would have paid for one that could see, and eventually he and his blind horse had made enough money to buy a small grocery store.

Home was a two-story frame house, and it was a warm and happy place. "I learned a great deal from my father," Eppie would recall for a *Chicago Tribune* reporter in 1990. "He would become one of the most respected citizens in the city. But there was more than respect. He was dearly loved by everybody. He had a special spark and a delicious sense of humor. He never met a stranger and he never met anyone he couldn't get along with. He was truly extraordinary, a real 'people person.' It was from him that I learned how to be a communicator. One of the things my father told me I have always remembered: 'You never learn anything while you're talking.'"

She considered her mother "a saint . . . the one who established the standards in our family. She provided the discipline and set the moral tone. She was a beautiful woman, loving but firm. There was never any question about where she stood. [Popo] and I could con Daddy and wrap him around our little fingers, but Mama—never. From her I learned a sense of responsibility and that no matter what, you kept your word."

The family was Jewish, and Eppie would later say she was "brought up to be proud of her Jewishness." Indeed, she would often refer to herself as "the Jewish Joan of Arc" and the "original square Jewish lady from Sioux City." Though millions of Americans knew her only by the Waspy Ann Landers name, she said that Jewish culture had something to do with her success as an advice columnist, "being sympathetic to other people and their problems, because the Jews through the centuries have been persecuted and have had great troubles and problems."

In 1930, when the twins were twelve, Abe Friedman sold his grocery store and bought a movie theater, made that successful, and then bought two more. "He owned every theater in town except the Orpheum," Eppie would often say, pride still in her voice decades later, adding that, "My father was one of the first theater owners to install popcorn machines and those machines took in more money than the box office."

The twins were inseparable. "I don't recall ever being alone with one or the other, because they were constantly together. And you just thought of them as one person," said first cousin Ruth Davidson in a 2000 episode of TV's *Biography* about Eppie.

They were also an aggressively playful pair. Exploiting their twinship in elementary school, they loved to switch places, which delighted classmates and infuriated teachers. Eppie was usually the instigator, easily convincing Popo to join in mischief. As Davidson recalled, "My parents, when they knew the twins were coming over, would say, 'Uh-oh. Lock everything up,' because you never knew what they were going to do. [Once] their grandfather was taking a nap on the sofa and they cut off his beard." Still, Eppie could remember getting spanked only once, after she and Popo used scissors to cut the fringe off some lamp shades and curtains in their living room.

If the twins were natural pranksters, they were also born performers. Their parents often allowed hoboes to move into the house and sleep in the basement, trading a roof and a few hot meals for yard work and odd chores. And though Eppie would later say on *Biography*, "There were four girls in the house and here was this tramp in the basement. I was just boggled," the twins used these "tramps" as a sort of captive audience when they wanted to display their abilities with a song or with the violin, which they both played.

They loved to perform, as another old friend recalled: "One day, not informing anybody, not being invited, they went down to the prison and played the violin for the prisoners. That was such an event that it made the newspapers."

In 1932, they entered Central High School, where, at least judging from their senior yearbook, they were popular. A large number of autographs from classmates pepper the book. Most are just signatures, some embellished by a " '36."

A few classmates were more wordy.

"To the sweetest gals in the world—Jean Fitzgerald."

"Dear 'Twins', Lots of luck, and may you always possess your super abundance of 'vim, vigor and vitality!' As ever, Marjorie Howard."

"Just one of the guys. Bob Rae. No love. No kisses."

One of the interesting things about the book, about all old yearbooks for that matter, is the list of activities in which the students participated. In the twins' yearbook you'd discover such familiar, almost timeless extracurricular activities as sports, band, chorus, debate, Honor Society, newspaper, chess, and foreign languages. But you'd also find four "literary" clubs (Erodelphian, Chrestomathian, Hesperian, and Elite), the Hi-Y ("To promote clean living, good morals, and high standards"), the Hi-Tri ("To make profitable contacts with the outside world, and to maintain high moral standards"), and the Marionette Club, whose members "wish to learn everything about the making and operating of marionettes."

Eppie apparently wasn't interested in marionettes, but she was a member of the Castle Commercial Club, Orchestra, Castle Kamera Club, Friendship Club, Dramatic Club, Parnasus ("a new club organized to promote good reading"), International Relations Club (Vice President), Art Club, and Spanish Club. Popo was a member of the same clubs, except for Friendship.

Eppie was also not interested in those traditional high school experiments, smoking and drinking, even though the twins were exposed to a relatively worldly crowd. "We got our sex education talking to the chorus girls" who performed burlesque at some of her father's theaters, Eppie said, on the eve of her eightieth birthday. "They were a pretty fast crowd, but at fifteen I made the firm decision to never use either alcohol or cigarettes. There was no horror story involved. I just thought that these were things I didn't have to get involved with. That decision served me well. I look at people my age and, well, they look a lot older."

All of the kids in the 1936 yearbook look so fresh and young that they seem ageless. But you know they will grow up, and you know that life will give them joys and problems, and you wonder what will happen, what did happen, to these kids. And you look for clues in the quotations underneath the photos of the seniors. They represent, in a sense, epitaphs for childhood, and though most are so simple—"Known for her dancing," "A great pal," "Blond and great," "Tall and very blond," "A friend worth having," "Always studying," "Always whistling," "Interested in sports," "This tall lady likes to skate," "A keen kid"—others make for wonder and worry, even more than sixty-five years later.

Wonder about the boy whose photo is accompanied by this quotation, "This 'Bill' comes oftener than once a month."

Worry about the student who inspired, "He seems to be slightly mixed up."

Wonder about another boy because, "He can never be dignified, guess why?"

Worry about the teenager who is "either tooting or on a toot."

Under Popo's photo is this: "Always with Eppie."

And under Eppie's is this: "Always with Po-Po."

"When I was a teenager (back in the Stone Age, of course) 13-year-old girls didn't wear nail polish, nylons, strapless evening gowns and lipstick," Eppie wrote in her 1963 book, *Ann Landers Talks to Teen-Agers About Sex*. "There wasn't the social pressure to 'grow up.' Our mothers didn't worry so much about whether or not we were popular. Back in the 1930s, mothers were worrying about other things."

After high school, the twins enrolled in Morningside College, a small Methodist-affiliated school in Sioux City. It covered almost thirty acres, and its eight hundred-some students paid $85 a semester. It's likely that the twins were better off financially than the other students, since their father's movie theaters were thriving. "[The twins] were robust but choice. The two girls were built like a brick outhouse. They showed up on [the Morningside] campus in a pair of skunk coats," said an anonymous Morningside alumnus in an unauthorized 1987 biography of the sisters, *Dear Ann, Dear Abby*. "The black and white stripes [of their coats] advertised them like road signs.

The two of them together were pretty startling; they were about as gaudy as you could get. They looked like a pair of angelfish."

Eppie and Popo majored in English and journalism. Decades later, Eppie didn't remember much about her college journalism courses. "Not a thing," she said. "I certainly never took those courses because I thought of a career in journalism. Popo and I were trying to take courses where the teachers had a reputation for being easy graders." And Popo recalled, "I was a good student because I knew getting good report cards was the way to please my parents. I avoided subjects that would pull down my grades, subjects like math and science."

Characteristically, they did not avoid the limelight, such as it was. They wrote a gossip column and submitted it to the campus newspaper, the *Collegian*. The "Campus Rat" carried the unusual byline "By Pe-ep" and then later, "By the Friedman Twins." A typical item: "B. and C. believe in pitching a little woo wherever and whenever they feel so inclined. . . . If we wanted to start up a good fuss, we could tell them that they had an audience."

Eppie rarely talked to me about her years at Morningside College. It would have been interesting to know more about "Campus Rat," in part because Eppie retained the taste for gossip. She was always asking me about the romantic lives of Chicago's reporters and socialites: Now, is so-and-so gay? What's the real scoop on that editor and his secretary?

But she never talked about "Campus Rat," about what it was like when she and Popo dated the editors of the *Collegian,* one of whom would later claim that Eppie and Popo "wanted to be notorious, in a positive sense. We helped them."

One fact about Eppie's and Popo's college days stayed constant though the years: Their interests were less academic than social. "We really majored in boys," Eppie said. And even in that pursuit, they were inseparable, though, as Eppie would later write, "Of course we were interested in sex. . . . But my generation was more self-conscious about it. In our day [we] hugged and kissed and called it necking."

A fellow named Henry Ginsburg recalled for *Biography* that, even though he might have been inflating the length of the "relationship," "in the four or five years that I dated Eppie, [I don't remember] ever going on a date with her alone, never. Always with Popo."

And as Eppie confirmed to a TV interviewer in 1978: "That was a pretty wild time, actually. A lot of kids were drinking. 'The roaring '30s.' That's when I grew up and I was not part of that. I was considered a prude. And I'm not ashamed of it, but I was never alone with a boy, always had to double-date with my twin sister. I mean, if a guy didn't have a friend for Sissy, no go. There is safety in numbers."

· LOT 2695 ·

Early correspondence to
Eppie Friedman Lederer

Eppie first set eyes on the man who would become her one and only husband when she was out with her sister shopping for bridal veils at Sioux City's T.S. Martin Department Store. The twins were, of course, planning a double wedding.

Popo was engaged to Morton Phillips, whom she had met when she was a freshman in college. Eppie had been invited by Henry Ginsburg to a fraternity dance at the University of Minnesota. Naturally, she would not go without her sister, so Ginsburg arranged a date for Popo. While she was dancing with her date, another fellow tapped the man's shoulder and asked to cut in. That was Phillips. He and Popo danced all night.

Phillips was a quiet sort, giving no initial hints that he was heir to a Minnesota-based family fortune. At the turn of the century, his father and uncle had started a newspaper delivery route and eventually expanded it to include the distribution throughout the Midwest of candy, cigars, tobacco, and other specialty items; the distribution and manufacture of liquor; and later the manufacture and sales of kitchen utensils and household appliances. The family was also active in many charitable and philanthropic ventures, funding medical research and health causes.

Eppie got engaged two years after Popo. The fiancé was Lewis Dreyer and she had met him during her junior year at college, when she and her family were vacationing in California. He was a law student at UCLA, and they met through connections in the movie business: Eppie's father owned theaters, and Dreyer's father was a vice president at RKO Pictures.

The double-wedding date had been set: July 2, 1939. But while she and Popo were shopping for their veils, Eppie met Jules Lederer. He was twenty-one, quick-witted, handsome, and, by circumstance, something of a hustler in the best sense of that often misused word.

Born in Detroit, he was the third of seven children. His father, Morris, was a Romanian immigrant who had grown up in Detroit and made his living as a traveling salesman, selling ladies' aprons and notions to stores throughout the Midwest. He often took young Jules with him on these trips, teaching him early in life the tricks and nuances of salesmanship. Those skills were employed prematurely after Morris was killed when the car he was driving was hit by a train. Dropping out of school in the tenth grade to help support the family, Jules got work as a stock boy. He worked running a freight elevator. He swept floors. But his bosses at Kern's Department Store sensed that this was a youngster born to sell and moved him into retailing. In short time he moved on to become an assistant manager of millinery at a store in Grand Rapids, living frugally so he could send much of his earnings home to help support his mother, Gustie. He later became manager of ladies' millinery at a store in Lansing. When he first set eyes on Eppie, he had just arrived in Sioux City.

One frequent feature of the "Ann Landers" column over the years was "how we met" letters, sentimental love stories that were eventually collected in book form. Many were set in the World War II years—"He was on leave and I was a waitress," sort of encounters, often with an O'Henry-esque twist.

Eppie's meeting Jules would certainly qualify for a "Best of How We Met":

"Dear Ann Landers: My twin sister and I were shopping for wedding veils for our upcoming double wedding and the salesman was this handsome young man who was kind of giving me the eye. As I went over to the mirror to see how I looked, he whispered to my twin sister, 'I'm very attracted to your sister but what can I do? I would like to ask her out to a dance but she's engaged.' My sister said, 'Ask her. What's the worst that can happen? She'll say no?' So, he comes up to me and says, 'You're the first girl I ever met that I wanted to marry. And you're coming in to buy a wedding veil.' But he asked me out anyway. I broke off my engagement, and we were happily married for thirty-six years."

This would have been a problem, if not a scandal, in the late 1930s. But after their first date, Eppie knew her marriage to Dreyer could not take place, and when she asked her father how and when to break things off with the West Coast fiancé, he said simply, "Better now than later." Abe Friedman no doubt liked Jules, sensing perhaps that they shared not only ambition but a rough charm and sense of humor. One story has it that the first time the two men met, Abe, initially skeptical that, because of his blond hair and Romanesque nose, Jules might not be Jewish, said, "Say something in Yiddish," and Jules replied, "I vanna go for a valk."

A few weeks later, Jules proposed, Eppie accepted, and two days before their twenty-first birthdays in 1939, Eppie and Popo, dressed in identical satin bridal gowns and each holding one of their father's arms, walked down the aisle of the Shaare-Zion Synagogue and were married in a ceremony so lavish for the time that it was covered by the local paper, which noted that mounted police were stationed outside to control a crowd of curious onlookers.

There were two hundred–some guests at the afternoon wedding, which was followed by dinner. Later, five hundred more people—friends, business associates, and other relatives—joined the party to share champagne toasts and cake in honor of the brides. The next day the couples took off on a double honeymoon, their first stop being Chicago, where they stayed in the fashionable pink stucco Edgewater Beach Hotel on the shore of Lake Michigan.

As Popo and Mort moved to Minneapolis and settled into the comfortable life befitting a young executive being groomed to take over a family business, Eppie and Jules moved into a one-bedroom apartment in Sioux City, $300 in debt. Jules was still employed selling hats and though he and Eppie were able to move into a larger apartment by the time their daughter, Margo, was born in March 1940, Eppie would later recall, "we lived with no luxuries at all, with no extra money for anything."

The family's life became nomadic, as better-paying sales opportunities lured Jules. In their first seven years of marriage, the family moved eight times. "I saw more of a moving van than I saw of my husband," Eppie would say, though she never complained. Her philosophy was "you go where the grapes grow," and that remained her way of thinking even after she became Ann Landers.

In 1942, having lived for a short time in St. Louis and then back in Sioux City, the family settled in New Orleans, where Jules went to work at the Marx Isaacs Department Store. Their stay was relatively lengthy and stable, coming to an end when Jules was drafted in 1944. By coincidence, he and Mort wound up stationed in the same infantry unit at Camp Robinson near Little Rock, Arkansas, where they would become close friends. But Eppie and Margo were forced to return to Sioux City and move in with Eppie's parents. And Eppie was at home the night her mother, Rebecca Friedman, returned ill from a neighbor's house and died of a cerebral hemorrhage. She was fifty-six. The family gathered for the funeral, Mort and Jules being given emergency leave, and within months, the war was over. Having gotten to know his brother-in-law well, Mort offered Jules a job selling pots and pans for a Phillips family–owned company called Guardian Services in Los Angeles. Jules jumped at it, and within a couple of years, he had moved to Chicago as district manager of Guardian. Six months later, when Mort moved to Eau Claire, Wisconsin, to become president of National Presto Industries, a kitchen appliance company owned by the Phillips family, he offered his brother-in-law a job there as vice president in charge of sales.

The twins' lives in Eau Claire were, at least on the surface, different. Popo and Mort lived in a large house with three full-time servants. Eppie, Jules, and Margo lived in a more modest house that Popo and Eppie referred to as "Peanut Place." Much has been made, through the years, about the economic and social disparity between the Phillipses and Lederers during these Eau Claire years, some people speculating that it fostered resentment and jealousy in Eppie and the need to get away from Eau Claire. But the sisters ran together in the town's small social circle, did volunteer work for various organizations, and, in varying ways, exhibited the same affection, playfulness, and togetherness they had always shared.

The twins devoted much of their time to working for charities and women's groups and with their husbands became part of the town's relatively small social scene. Their kids also got together often. Margo says that she spent a lot of time at Popo's house because "there were so many things to do over there."

There were also two cousins, Jeanne, two years younger than Margo, and Edward, five years younger. The two girls played together, sometimes putting on their mothers' high heels and trying to dance. They would laugh and giggle playing grown-up. "Jeanne and I . . . were friends and did many thing together," Margo recalled. "I was the elder, so of course there was a bit of worship going on, which I thought made for a very fine friendship."

Jeanne remembered "Margo coming over to our house when we were kids, but I don't recall us playing dress-up. I do remember that she had a terrible asthma attack once. I do know that I always looked up to her. She was sophisticated. Me? She probably thought I was a pain in the butt."

3

· LOT 2602 ·

Koerner. American Twentieth Century.
A Portrait of Hubert Humphrey

In an essay written long before the country would become cynical about politics and politicians, Hubert Humphrey wrote, "If young men and women are seeking a real challenge, if they want to do things with their lives that matter, then a career in politics and government has the potential that cannot be matched in any other endeavor."

Before she would get to know Humphrey, Eppie might well have been the living embodiment of those words. Her political activism was sparked by the communist-baiting, alcoholic demagogue Joseph McCarthy, the U.S. senator from Wisconsin who began his loud, messy, and damaging activities in 1950.

"I sensed that this was an evil and dangerous man," Eppie said. "And I thought something should be done about it."

Eppie's friend Edna "Blondie" Brigham was of similar mind, recalling on *Biography*: "Eppie and I both felt strongly that [McCarthy's] tactics were rather villainous. Maybe we weren't smart enough to be afraid. We were writing radio scripts, developing telephone campaigns, and canvassing neighborhoods [to help defeat McCarthy in the 1952 Senate election] . . . Everything that we really didn't know much about."

But Eppie was a quick study, and it became immediately apparent that politics was able to provide not only a means for her to satisfy her desire to do good for the community but also to feed the ego and ambition not sated by volunteer work. Politics was exciting, stimulating, challenging. She was hardly acting the conventional role of 1950s wife and mother but rather displaying the fierce independence and feisty spirit that would characterize the rest of her life. Insatiably curious, irresistibly charming, and quick-witted, she was someone to be reckoned with, and it is likely that had she not gone on to become one of the world's most famous newspaper columnists, she would have made a large mark in some other field.

Her personality and activism, especially in a predominantly Republican town like Eau Claire, attracted a lot of attention and allowed for the first of what would become frequent visits to Washington, D.C. There Eppie charmed a variety of power brokers and politicians, starting what would be lifelong friendships.

Most notable among the politicians was Humphrey, then a bright young senator from Minnesota who would go on to serve as vice president, run unsuccessfully for president, and introduce Eppie to virtually every important Democrat in Washington.

"He was a dear friend of mine," Eppie said after Humphrey died in 1977. "I knew Hubert and [his wife] Muriel well over thirty years. They were wonderful people and I miss Hubert every day of my life. I miss his voice. I used to talk to him on the phone very often and see him and Muriel frequently. They were dear, close friends. The last thing that Hubert wrote was the essay for my [1978 best-selling] book, *The Ann Landers Encyclopedia A to Z*. It is called 'Politics As a Career' because he loved politics. He respected it, felt that people should know that it isn't the dirty, grubby, corrupt business that a great many people think it is."

Though McCarthy won reelection in 1952 (he would, two years later, be censured by the Senate and, disgraced and drinking with increasing vigor, die in 1957), in the fall of 1953, Eppie was asked to become chair of the Eau Claire County Democratic Party, a volunteer position appointed by the county's Democratic Committee. She accepted the offer but was soon embroiled in a dirty and grubby election. Opposition to her appointment was mounted by some disgruntled members of the party who decided to slate their own candidate, an attorney for the Steelworkers Union. That was the union that represented the employees at Presto, which was owned by Mort's family and where Jules worked, turning the race into a battle between the union man and the executive's wife.

Mort and Jules remained apart from the election ("I had the

freedom to do what I wanted to do, and did it," Eppie said), which smacked of Chicago-style politics involving charges and countercharges of vote fraud, backroom maneuvers, and a revote. Eventually, Eppie won the post, but her victory and position could hardly have prepared her for the rough-and-tumble of real politics in Chicago, with its cigar-chomping, pinky-ring-wearing boodlers and bandits. That's where Eppie, Jules, and Margo moved in the summer of 1954. It was a relocation prompted primarily by Jules's ambition but also fueled by the desires he and Eppie shared to get out of the shadows cast by Mort and Popo, and to live in a more sophisticated, urban place.

In Chicago, Jules quickly found a job as president of a company called Autopoint, which made ballpoint pens and pencils that could be turned into promotional items, emblazoned with company names or personal messages. The family had lived in Chicago once before, during the early years of the marriage, as Jules moved his family across the country seeking better-paying sales jobs. It was familiar territory to them since also, while living in Eau Claire, Eppie would frequently hop the train into the city, with Popo and often with Margo as well, for one- or two-day shopping trips.

The family moved into a three-bedroom apartment at 1000 Lake Shore Drive, at the corner of Oak Street. It was one of the city's most prominent buildings, situated in an area called the Gold Coast. The building had—still has—a magnificent view of the lake to the east and the crescent-shaped stretch of sand known as Oak Street Beach. This would always be Eppie's slice of the city, and even after forty years of living there, she was still smitten. "I travel a lot because of my work, and I love it," she told a *Chicago Tribune* reporter in 1990. "But when I'm away, I miss my apartment and I miss the city. When I walk in my front door, I kiss the walls I'm so glad to be home."

But during her first few months living in Chicago, she was bored. Jules was working long hours in his new job. Margo was making new friends and adjusting to high school life at Francis Parker, a private school a few miles north, so close to the Lincoln Park Zoo that kids on the school's playing fields could hear the roar of lions.

Eppie desperately wanted to stay in politics, and she believed she could. A story in the *Eau Claire Leader-Telegram* bidding her farewell warned Chicago to "watch out for Eppie Lederer— she'll make her mark on the city." So, in the fall of 1954, it was a confident woman who sat down across the desk from Jacob Arvey, one of Chicago's go-to guys, a man with the connections and influence—the "clout"—to do favors, get jobs, make or break careers.

Arvey was boss of Chicago's "Democratic Machine," the Cook County Democratic Committee, which carried with it effective control of the state party and a leading national-party role. His most notable successes came in 1948, when he arranged for the party to nominate Paul Douglas, a distinguished university economist, for U.S. senator, and Adlai Stevenson for governor. Arvey was a powerful force in the maneuverings that led four years later to Stevenson's "draft" as the Democratic presidential candidate.

Both the Democratic and Republican National Conventions were held in Chicago in 1952, the first to be broadcast on national TV. In July, the Republicans picked the Dwight Eisenhower– Richard Nixon ticket. A month later Eppie was on hand as a delegate from Wisconsin when the Democrats selected the ticket of Stevenson and John Sparkman. It was there that she beguiled CBS television's Walter Cronkite, who would become a life-long friend and, for a time, "the most trusted man in America." As a testimonial to the kind of drive and spark Eppie possessed long before she became Ann Landers, Cronkite recalled for *Biography* that at the Democratic convention "I was immediately struck with the effervescence of this woman. As I recall, I fought my way through the admiring crowd until I got up close enough to meet her."

It is likely that Eppie believed that "effervescence" would have a positive effect on Arvey. There have been, over the years, in interviews and books, a number of versions of their 1954 conversation. Whatever the precise wording, Arvey's message to the thirty-six-year-old housewife from Wisconsin was clear:

- I don't think you're going to fit in here. You come from an idealistic place.
- You're too independent. If you saw things you didn't like, you'd raise hell and we don't need any more hell-raisers.
- [You want to be a] national committeewoman? Forget it. Take up golf. There are hundreds of women more qualified.
- If you persist, I will worry that you might wind up in Lake Michigan wearing a cement ankle bracelet.

Eppie must have been very disappointed. She would have to find something else to do. Luckily, there were opportunities. Of all the cities in which the family might have settled, none could have been more potentially nurturing for ambition than Chicago.

In 1955, *Fortune* magazine took a look at America, focusing on Chicago and observing, "Right now the most exciting city in the U.S. is Chicago, Illinois. What is happening in Chicago amounts, in many ways, to a rebuilding in the worst way; it is getting it in a big way. . . . All over the city there is a fury of blasting and leveling. And, as the girders go up for the new over-passes, office buildings, factories, apartments, stores, and hospitals, even the most skeptical Chicagoan, hardened against mere rhetoric during the decades of tub-thumping, must now conclude that the city means business."

How easy it is now to look back at the 1950s as "the good old days." "Economically, the 1950s were certainly better, for most," wrote Alan Ehrenhalt in his 1995 sociological study *The Lost City: Discovering the Forgotten Virtues of Community in the Chicago of the 1950s*. "It was a time of unexpected prosperity. 'I've got a house, a new Chevy. Whoever would have believed it?' It was a time when one could live a comfortable middle-class life on one income; could play with all sorts of new toys that made life easier—TVs, dishwashers, air conditioning. There was an optimism, especially economic, that does not exist today. Read the articles of the time and they talk about finding a cure for cancer in 10 years."

The fifties certainly seemed a time of optimism for the Lederers. With Jules's new high-level position and Chicago's urbane setting, the family had luxuries and a lifestyle not available to them before. But with her political aspirations dampened by Arvey, Eppie was eager to find some other outlet for her energies. She had become a voracious newspaper reader in Eau Claire, believing it the best way to gain insight into the community, and she spent each Chicago morning engrossed with the local papers, particularly the *Chicago Sun-Times*. One of four newspapers of any consequence in the city, it was a morning tabloid, Democratic in its politics, which appealed to Eppie. And, thanks to Margo, Eppie knew Wilbur Munnecke, the paper's vice president and business manager.

They had met in the club car of a train traveling from Eau Claire to Chicago in 1952. Margo was only twelve, but precocious. She struck up a conversation with Munnecke and invited him to dinner. Eppie joined them, of course, and a friendship was kindled—and one new subscriber to the *Sun-Times* was realized when the Lederers moved to Chicago two years later.

One of the features in the *Sun-Times* that particularly intrigued Eppie was a four-day-a-week column that ran under the title "Your Problems" and carried the byline Ann Landers. It had first run in the *Chicago Sun* and the name Ann Landers was trademarked four years later when the *Sun* merged with the *Times*. It consisted of letters from people with a variety of problems, and answers from Landers. It was popular in the Lederer household.

More than forty years later, asked what she liked about that column, Eppie said, "I don't remember it that well, but it wasn't very snappy." But she did remember calling Munnecke one morning in 1955 and offering to help Ann Landers open and answer her mail.

· LOT 243C ·

"The Ann Landers Encyclopedia"

As long as there have been problems ("That guy in the next cave keeps borrowing my rocks and won't give them back. What should I do?"), there have been people willing to offer advice ("Hit him with one of those rocks the next time he comes over."), there have been people willing to offer advice ("Hit him with one of those rocks the next time he comes over.").

But for millennia, "professional" advice—advice that came from people who were paid to share their opinions about your problems—was available primarily to pharaohs, popes, and kings. Only recently, within the last century or so, has it been available—for a price—from analysts in fifty-minute "hour" increments. Of course, free advice could always be had from tavern keepers, clergymen, neighbors, parents, or pals. Newspapers got into the racket when the *London Journal* began running what it called a "lovelorn column" in the 1850s. Its anonymous columnist offered this advice to a woman named Annie V: "You must be cautious. Your lover evidently does not respect his future bride. The asp lurks beneath the flowers."

The U.S. newspaper advice column has its roots in the final decades of the 1800s, when newspapers, incorporating circulation-building novelties such as comics into their pages, also started featuring columns that addressed the concerns of the lovelorn and the otherwise troubled. This was a great period of invention for newspapers, which were trying to bulk up circulation. There is no way to pinpoint the appearance of the first printed U.S. advice column. No matter the date, it was not created as an altruistic public service but rather as an attraction for those seeking diversion.

Though some late-nineteenth-century papers carried what were called "correspondents' columns" under such pseudonyms as Sister Mary and Aunt Margaret, the advice business really took off in 1901, when several newspapers started running a syndicated advice column written by Elizabeth Meriwether Gilmer, a reporter for *The Daily Picayune* in New Orleans. As was the custom for women in the business at the time, she had chosen an alliterative pseudonymous byline, Dorothy Dix, and she proved adept and clever in addressing the problems of ordinary people.

Born near Woodstock, Tennessee, on November 18, 1870, Elizabeth received little formal schooling before her marriage in 1888 to an ill-fated fellow named George O. Gilmer. A short time after the marriage, he became mentally ill and was incapacitated until his death in an asylum. Forced to support herself, Gilmer suffered a nervous collapse. During her convalescence she began writing stories and sketches of life in her native Tennessee. In 1896 one of them attracted the notice of a neighbor, the owner of the *Picayune,* who offered her a job as a reporter. In addition to her reporting chores, also written under the byline Dorothy Dix, she began writing a Sunday advice column for women called "Sunday Salad."

The column was an instant success, and in a short time Gilmer became editor of the women's department and assistant to the editor of the paper. In 1901 she accepted a lucrative offer from William Randolph Hearst, that great thief of other papers' most talented writers, to move to his *New York Journal.* There she continued her column, now called "Dorothy Dix Talks," expanding from one to three days a week while also working as a reporter specializing in sex-scandal-murder stories. Gilmer gave up the reporter's life in 1917, leaving Hearst and joining the Wheeler Syndicate, to devote her energies full-time to her column, which was expanded to six days a week. She was dubbed "Mother Confessor to Millions," and many believed that her only serious rival in the field was Beatrice Fairfax, a pseudonym for a woman whose real name would have seemed perfectly alliterative for a byline, Marie Manning.

Born in Washington, D.C., probably in 1873 (the year is not certain), Manning was something of a well-to-do intellectual and received her education in New York City and London. It must have disappointed and even pained her parents greatly that her ambition was to become a newspaperwoman, an aspiration that, at the time, would have been a calling deemed only some-what higher than that of chorus girl. Her chance came at a Washington, D.C., dinner party where she met and obviously charmed an editor at the *New York World*. At his invitation she went to New York and took a job at space rates, meaning she was paid only for the quantity of submitted material that was actually printed. An exclusive interview with President Grover Cleveland shortly afterward won Manning a regular staff position.

In 1897 she joined Hearst's *Journal* where, after a year or so of turning out standard women's-page fare and covering sensational crime stories, she started writing an advice column under the byline of Beatrice Fairfax, a name she had compounded from Dante's Beatrice and Fairfax County, Virginia, where her family owned a home.

Within a few years, letters were arriving at the rate of more than a thousand a day. Questions concerning the finer points of courtship—how to win a man, how to hold a woman, what little intimacies were allowable in various circumstances—apparently troubled or at least interested thousands of readers. Fairfax's replies relied generally on a firm code of etiquette and the motto "Dry your eyes, roll up your sleeves, and dig for a practical solution." Manning would give up the column in 1905, resuming it in 1929 after being wiped out in the stock market crash; but it never regained the popularity it had at the turn of the century.

Another very different but influential advice column made its debut in 1906 in the *Jewish Daily Forward*. It was called "A Bintel Brief" ("A Bundle of Letters"), a forum in which readers could seek advice and support. The letters consisted of cries for help from the very poor, those who had problems dealing with religious discrimination, and people seeking advice in marriage or job decisions.

The editor of the paper for the first half of the twentieth century was Abraham Cahan, who often wrote the column. In his 1929 memoirs he observed that the column was popular because: "People often [need] the opportunity to be able to pour out their heavy-laden hearts. Among our immigrant masses this need was very marked. Hundreds of thousands of people, torn from their homes and their dear ones, were lonely souls who thirsted for expression, who wanted to hear an opinion, who wanted advice in solving their weighty problems. The 'Bintel Brief' created just this opportunity for them."

Eppie certainly would have been aware of "Bintel Brief," and though she would never be thought of by most of her readers as Jewish, she would ever possess the qualities of the stereotypical Jewish mother. She was doting. She was blunt. She was concerned. She could be a bit overbearing, always confident in the advice she dispensed.

But before Eppie's "Ann Landers" and Popo's "Dear Abby," Dorothy Dix would be remembered as the most famous advice columnist. At the height of the column's popularity in the 1930s, it was syndicated in three hundred–plus papers and had a readership of around 60 million. "I had greatly admired Dorothy Dix," Eppie would tell me. "[She was] the grandmother of advice columnists."

Gilmer never stopped writing as Dorothy Dix. She moved from syndicate to syndicate, also writing books with such titles as 1939's *How to Win and Hold a Husband*. She died in New Orleans,

Louisiana, on December 16, 1951. In a rare interview in 1947, Gilmer told Chicago columnist Irv Kupcinet, "[The times] decidedly have [changed]. I can recall many years ago when girls would write to ask if it was proper for them to help a gentleman on with his coat. Now they write to ask if it would be permissible for them to go on a weekend trip with their boyfriends."

Kupcinet, who would later become a colleague and close friend of Eppie's, asked the octogenarian Gilmer about the origins of her column name and she told him, "I always liked the name Dorothy, so I took it. As for Dix, my colored nanny always used to call her husband 'Mr. Dix.' I liked the alliteration. I've been offered huge sums of money for the name but I prefer when I die, Dorothy Dix goes with me."

Kupcinet also asked Gilmer what letter she most remembered. "Naturally," she said, "I'll never forget a lot of them. But I do recall one I didn't print. It was from a young girl who'd been married only a few weeks when she and her husband separated. Now she wanted a divorce. She wrote to me, not for advice about that, though, but to ask me to help her with another little problem she had. She couldn't remember her husband's name."

By the time Kupcinet interviewed Gilmer, readership for all advice columns was on a steady decline that had begun in the late 1930s and continued into the 1940s. How important did matters such as kissing on a first date seem in the midst of world war and unspeakable atrocities?

In the late 1940s, some newspaper syndicates had stopped offering advice columns altogether, and those columnists who remained in the field were far from being household names. One of the few who was well-known was Ann Landers, whose real name was Ruth Crowley. After Eppie's death, Crowley's name surfaced in a few of the obituaries. That prompted *San Francisco Chronicle* columnist Patricia Holt to detail some of the particulars of Crowley's life, bringing them to public attention for the first time.

"My heart always swells whenever reporters mention Ruth [Holt] Crowley," Holt wrote. "A registered nurse who specialized in baby care after World War II, she was my father's sister and much loved by my brother and me. By the time we were old enough to read a newspaper, Aunt Ruth had started both an advice column for new mothers at the *Chicago Sun-Times* and an afternoon TV show about raising babies. . . .

"Viewers and readers responded so enthusiastically to Aunt Ruth's amusing and no-nonsense answers to their queries that they began asking about other concerns, such as errant husbands, difficult in-laws, sibling rivalry.

"Soon the audience swelled to the point that Aunt Ruth's editors asked if she would be interested in writing a second column under a different name. Ann Landers, a friend of Aunt Ruth and her husband, my uncle Bill, willingly gave her name to the project, and voilà, the new Ann Landers column was born.

"To say it was an instant success would be the understatement of the 1950s. In Aunt Ruth's day, when a woman asked for advice about, say, a drunken and abusive husband, most lovelorn columnists would say something like this: 'Ah, marriage, so blessed yet sometimes so painful. Remember, a wife's duty is to be sympathetic to her struggling husband. Come, pray for him and find a way to stand by him as loving soul mate.'

"But this was outmoded 'Dorothea [*sic*] Dix stuff' to Aunt

Ruth, who would sum up her answer about the abusive husband in two words: 'Lose him.' Her boldness was such hot stuff in the 1950s that Ann Landers soon became syndicated throughout the country. . . .

"When the Crowleys came to visit us [in San Francisco], Dad and Uncle Bill would take our cousins and us fishing while Aunt Ruth worked on her column in my brother's room. Mom, sitting on a bed covered with mail, always wondered how people could send questions about personal problems 'to a stranger.'

"Aunt Ruth rarely responded to questions like that. She was so busy answering letters as Ann Landers, writing the baby column, doing her TV show and raising three kids that she just burrowed in and got the work done. Often when the mail built up, her teenage daughter Diane helped sort, file, brainstorm, and telephone various experts whom Aunt Ruth had painstakingly sought out.

"Ruth Crowley never had the searing wit of Eppie Lederer. . . . Of course, with the passing of Eppie Lederer, whom I admired greatly, it saddens me that few writers will ever mention Ruth Crowley again. But the creation of 'Ann Landers' is such an American story that I feel a certain jubilance will always remain . . . the spirit of building a better mousetrap/advice column/book review/household/law practice/family legacy never seems to flag, is somehow in our genes. So before they're packed up and sent to their respective places in history, here's to the Ruth Crowleys and Eppie Lederers of the world."

· LOT 2761 ·

Cadillac Brougham—License
"AL 1955"

I n some now-forgotten town in America in the mid-1950s, a woman had a walnut tree that was very close to her neighbor's property. Most of the walnuts were falling onto the neighbor's lawn and the neighbor was helping herself, gathering the nuts and taking them inside her house, perhaps to eat, maybe to make a pie. Who knows? The two ladies exchanged harsh words about the nuts, but the matter remained unresolved. So the woman who owned the walnut tree decided to seek some advice from an outside source. She sat down and wrote a letter to a newspaper columnist named Ann Landers.

Meanwhile, in another now-forgotten city, another woman needed help. She was Catholic and her fiancé was Protestant. This was causing friction between the families of the two love-birds, prompting all manner of troubles and questions, including arguments about which church would be the setting for the nuptials. One morning she sat down and wrote to Ann Landers, whose advice column was carried by her local newspaper.

There were still four major newspapers in Chicago in 1955. The *Tribune* was by far dominant, with a circulation of 907,570. The *Daily News* had 591,341 and its afternoon rival the *American* 524,656. The *Sun-Times* had 556,885. Eppie was an avid newspaper reader, so it's likely that her feelings about the newspaper business were closer to the high-minded sentiments of playwright Arthur Miller ("A good newspaper is a nation talking to itself") or legendary Chicago editor Wilbur Storey ("It is the newspaper's duty to print the news and raise hell") than to those of the city's mayor at the time, Richard J. Daley, who said, "A newspaper is the lowest thing there is."

When she arrived at the *Sun-Times* offices in August 1955, Eppie had already been told by Munnecke that the woman who wrote the "Ann Landers" column, Ruth Crowley, had died on July 16 and that the paper was in the midst of seeking a replacement. The column was syndicated to a couple of dozen other newspapers. Writing it was a coveted job. At the time, most female journalists—what few there were—were relegated to the so-called women's pages, covering society events, flower and garden shows, and fashion shows. Writing an advice column, a task that combined a chance to be playful and the belief that one was doing some good by helping people with their problems, was such a prize that ten thousand women had applied to take the place of Dorothy Dix when she died in 1951.

The *Sun-Times*'s efforts to fill the Ann Landers job were not made public, so fewer than thirty women already affiliated with the newspaper business were vying for the job, some with journalistic experience, others married to the paper's executives.

Though Eppie had little experience as a writer or an advice-giver, save for the parental variety she was likely doling out to her teenage daughter, she was given the chance to enter the contest. Munnecke was, after all, one of the top men at the *Sun-Times,* and by this time a close family friend of the Lederers'. He had helped select the private school Margo was attending and introduced Eppie and Jules to some of the city's prominent citizens.

So it was no big deal for Munnecke to arrange for Eppie to become one of the candidates for the Ann Landers job, but then she would be on her own. Eppie would always appreciate this gesture of friendship. As she would later write about Munnecke, "I would like to give a very special halo for his special guidance. Will's insight and his mature approach to living have a stabilizing effect on those fortunate enough to be counted as his friends."

Munnecke arranged for Eppie to meet the man in charge of finding the new Ann Landers and the person who would eventually be her boss. Larry Fanning had joined the *Sun-Times* only six months earlier, as the editor of the *Sun-Times* syndicate, but had been in the business for two decades. Born in Minneapolis in 1914, he began his career in San Francisco, becoming the managing editor of the *San Francisco Chronicle* at twenty-seven. He came to Chicago with his wife of three years, Virginia Nissen, known to everyone as Ginny.

Fanning was balding, his remaining hair close-cropped. His glasses were black and thick and always perched halfway down his nose. At the office, he always wore a bowtie and crisp, button-down shirts. He was always smoking a pipe and had a laugh that boomed with a pleasant urgency. He asked Eppie, "Do you have any samples of your writing?" Eppie said, "I won a high school essay contest and I write to my parents almost every day and they think the letters are wonderful. I write them some poems that I call Eppie-grams."

Under different circumstances, Fanning might have given such a person a quick brush-off: "Is this some kind of joke?" Maybe he was courteous for Munnecke's sake. Or perhaps he was charmed by Eppie's personality. He would not have been the first or the last to be so affected.

"He asked me all sorts of questions, and what I told Larry was that the column wasn't about scrapbooks or psychology. It was about helping people, and all I wanted was a chance," Eppie told me about her first meeting with Fanning.

At the end of that meeting, Fanning handed her a stack of letters that made up the contest packet and told Eppie to take them home and answer them as best she could. Eppie went to work immediately.

A number of the women involved would later report that the contest was "blind," with each applicant given a letter code. Eppie told me she could not remember such a code and neither could another applicant—my mother. In an interesting twist of fate, my mother, Marilew, was one of those in the contest. She was thirty-six and had two children under five—me and my brother, Mark. Fanning and *Sun-Times* editor Milburn "Pete"

Akers suggested that she enter. "It wasn't a frivolous offer," my mother told me. "I was working at the Art Institute. I'd just taken over its public relations department, but I had a lot of newspaper experience. I'd worked at the *Tribune*, starting in the late thirties, the youngest person on the whole staff. I did a lot of things there. Your dad wasn't particularly enthusiastic about my getting in the contest. I knew some of the other women involved, but at that time I had never even heard of Eppie. So I took the sample questions and answered them, just off the top of my head. In the end, Pete and Larry said my answers were just too flip."

Eppie provided answers for all of the letters, but the two that have taken on almost mythic relevance were those from the woman with the walnut tree and the woman with the interfaith-marriage dilemma.

On the walnut matter, she reportedly called Supreme Court Justice William O. Douglas, whom she had met in Washington through Hubert Humphrey. She explained to Douglas what she was doing. He told her that he would have a clerk do some research and that he would get back to her in fifteen minutes. He did and the answer was this: The woman on whose lawn the walnuts were falling could eat them, cook them, or give them to friends, but she could not sell them.

Eppie asked Douglas if she could use his name as her authority.

"If it will help, go ahead," he said.

As for the interfaith-marriage letter, Eppie called another acquaintance, Father Theodore Hesburgh, the president of the University of Notre Dame, whom she had met at a convention she attended with Jules some years before, a gathering of young and influential business, political, and religious leaders. He would become one of her closest friends and most trusted advisers. It was a relationship she would one day characterize to a reporter as "the greatest unfertilized romance in the history of the world." He would later say of her that she was "never bashful about anybody . . . not awed by presidents, college presidents, or presidents of countries. She was always very quick at making friends. From the very beginning she was very open, very friendly, and very uninhibited. I think it's just part of her personality."

Hesburgh listened to the question and said, "[The couple] can be married in the Catholic Church, but the Protestant man will have to take instructions from a priest and promise to raise the children as Catholics."

Eppie asked Hesburgh if she could use his name as her authority.

"Yes," he said.

A few days later, Eppie returned to the *Sun-Times* with the letters and her responses. Fanning took a look and said, "You can't use these people's names. Justice Douglas and Father Hesburgh! They'll sue us."

When Eppie told Fanning that she actually knew these people and they had given her permission to use their names, Fanning asked, "How long do you think you could keep this up?" and Eppie told him, "I think I can keep it up for quite a while."

Fanning gave her another batch of letters and told Eppie to answer them and return the next day with her replies, which she did. By then the field of candidates had narrowed to only a few, which included Eppie and my mother. It's rumored that these finalists had to take a written psychological test, but neither Eppie nor my mother could recall having taken one. In any case, Fanning, Munnecke, and other key editors sat down to make their final decision. It was on a Monday morning in September 1955 that the paper's owner, Marshall Field IV, had his secretary dial a number.

"It's ringing," she said.

Field picked up the receiver in his office and heard Eppie Lederer say, "Hello."

"Good morning, Ann Landers," said Field.

Jamie O'Reilly

SINGER / SONGWRITER

Chicago

I was to sing at a dinner in 1986 honoring the retirement of Father Theodore Hesburgh from Notre Dame. The gala was held at the Chicago Hilton. Comedian Tom Dreesen was the featured act for the evening. That night, I was especially nervous. I was dressed in a new knockoff pink taffeta bridesmaid dress, sweating and nauseous, trying to pull in my newly pregnant tummy in front of all these distinguished people and society ladies in their beautiful gowns.

I was to be introduced after Tom's performance and then sing "Rose of Tralee" and other Irish songs, accompanied on piano by my oldest girlfriend, Pat Preston, with whom I'd won a sixth-grade talent show at St. Thomas the Apostle School. (We split the $5 prize.) Tom really wowed the crowd with Chicago stories and jokes told in his slick Las Vegas style. He sure knew how to work a crowd. At the time he was the opening act for Frank Sinatra whenever Sinatra went on tour.

So there I come out onstage feeling as awkward as I have ever felt onstage and I'm looking out over this vast crowd of tuxedos and sequins and I'm trying to find at least one face I know. That's what I sometimes do onstage to get my bearings: find the face of a friend.

But I don't see anybody and I feel like I should, could, just jump off the stage, and hide under a table when I see Ann Landers sitting there at one of the front tables. I knew her mostly by her hair. That was the most unmistakable "do." And what's she doing? She's smiling at me, sending me this "Go get 'em, kid" kind of vibe, and I think she maybe even winked at me.

I forgot all about how I looked and where I was and I think I sang pretty well after that. The crowd was applauding wildly, and so I sang "Danny Boy," my surefire, signature tune, and the crowd liked that too. It made Father Hesburgh cry, and I could see Ann Landers clapping like crazy and then winking at me—that time I was sure she winked at me.

During his speech, Father Hesburgh got very sentimental talking about his mother and how much she loved Irish songs. I just stood off to the side of the stage listening to him. And I started to think about what was really going on: how so long ago Father Hesburg helped get Ann Landers her job by answering one of her test questions when she got the column. I don't how I knew that story but I did. And I started to think that if he hadn't done that then she wouldn't have been here and she wouldn't have been Ann Landers looking at me and helping me get through the night. It all seemed too perfect.

Marilyn (Mare) Kirschenbaum

VP—INFLAMMATORY BREAST CANCER
RESEARCH FOUNDATION

Chicago

I n the late 1950s I didn't know of anyone who hadn't read "Ann Landers." It was the "in" thing to do. After I graduated from high school, I worked at a newspaper/radio advertising company in downtown Chicago and in the summertime, a group of coworkers and I sat on one of the tour boats that were docked in the river. Every day we'd have lunch there, read Ann Landers, and discuss her responses, sometimes getting into heated conversations. Every column was completely different and sometimes we found the questions strange, but Ann Landers always treated her readers with respect. In print she never acted like she was above anyone else. And her humor would crack us up.

I continued to be a loyal reader after I got married and had two daughters. In 1997, my elder daughter, Karen, discovered a large mass in her breast that had appeared suddenly.

She was first diagnosed with infiltrating ductal adenocarci-
noma. A few days prior to her scheduled surgery, she complained about her breast being warm to the touch and noticed
some wrinkling around the areola area. A new diagnosis
determined that she had something called inflammatory
breast cancer. Surgery was immediately cancelled because the
first protocol for IBC is chemotherapy. Fortunately, she
responded to her treatments, and six years later continues to
do amazingly well.

That was the first I had heard of IBC, the most aggressive
type of breast cancer. In August 1997, I became involved with
an Internet-based e-mail list that focused on education and
emotional support for patients with IBC, their friends, and
their families. We were just a grassroots effort.

Things changed dramatically after a letter appeared in the
"Ann Landers" column in May 1999. The column detailed the
symptoms of the disease and mentioned it by name. When I
saw that letter, there were screams of joy. I lost my voice
because of all the phone calls I made spreading the word. My
fingers cramped writing so many e-mails letting people know.
I was delirious with happiness because I knew that the article,
unbeknownst to Ann Landers, was going to save lives.

My husband and I went on a driving vacation shortly after
the column appeared. We knew the general public had never
heard of IBC. Leaving copies of the column would attract a
lot of attention; you'd have to live in a cave not to know who
Ann Landers was! But what better way to let them know
about it than by posting her column everyplace? It was then
the only piece of literature out available for laypeople.

We posted the columns in bathrooms and in gambling

casinos. We'd hand them to waitresses in restaurants, put piles of copies in stores, department stores, supermarkets, and museums, and we put copies of that column on bulletin boards in hotels. We left piles of them in gas stations. You name it!

This was the beginning. The IBC Research Foundation was founded a couple of months later. Ann Landers's article gave us the impetus and so there is no doubt that she helped save so many lives and continues to do so. I wish I had had the pleasure of meeting and thanking her in person. She was a lady in every sense of the word and what a great contribution she made in the world with her warmth, knowledge, and determination. Many people will remember Ann Landers as an important part of twentieth-century history. To me she was an angel.

Hugh M. Hefner

EDITOR–PUBLISHER

Los Angeles

I remember Ann Landers before she was Ann Landers. By that I mean that I can remember the column even before Eppie started writing it.

The woman who had been writing the "Ann Landers" column passed away, and one of the people recruited to help fill in until they found a permanent replacement was a woman I was dating, a very nice woman named Connie Chancellor. She had been married to a local TV newsman named John Chancellor, who would later become the NBC network anchor, and she had been working as a stringer for Kup [*Sun-Times* gossip columnist Irv Kupcinet] and so she knew a lot of the people at the paper.

I don't remember the first time I met Eppie. I was very busy in 1955. I had started *Playboy* less than two years before and we were all working virtually around the clock in offices across from Holy Name Cathedral. But Eppie and I met early on, almost certainly in 1956, and we became very good friends. It might seem unlikely to many people now, but Eppie and I shared similar views on a number of subjects such as gun control and human sexuality. We both believed that whatever went on in the bedroom between consenting adults was natural and healthy. That was, in the 1950s, something that people only whispered about if they talked about it at all.

We used to occasionally appear together on local TV talk shows and the only time we really disagreed about something was on one of those shows, when the topic was marijuana. I was for decriminalization of the drug and she was not. I think it quite interesting, and I think it says a great deal about Eppie's ability to change with the times, that she eventually softened her views on this issue and wound up decades later in favor of decriminalization.

She often came over to the *Playboy* mansion. [Written in Latin on a plaque above the doorbell at the mansion at 1340 N. State Parkway in Chicago, was a phrase that meant in English, "If you don't swing, don't ring."] She and her husband, Jules, would come over for Sunday dinners and to watch movies and she was always the first person to write a thank-you note. After I moved from Chicago to California in 1971, Eppie still called every once in a while and frequently sent me notes and letters. She remained a good friend and became a very good friend of my daughter Christie [who still lives in Chicago and is chairman and CEO of *Playboy*].

Personally I found Eppie charming and a loyal friend. A dear lady. She was the kind of person who should have been giving advice to the nation, a person with a good mind and her feet planted firmly on the ground. She helped open up a healthy dialogue about sex and relationships by raising topics in her column that had never before appeared in "family newspapers." She, her voice, and her opinions were so accepted in more conservative areas of the country, where wives and mothers respected her. In many places she was the only liberal voice that people heard. Without question she helped shape for the better the social and sexual landscape of this country.

Pat Collins

RETIRED FINANCIAL
COUNSELOR

Oak Lawn, Illinois

I had a sleeping problem from the time I was eighteen. I just thought I wasn't getting enough sleep. I worked for the FBI and falling asleep at work was a no-no. The first time it happened, in 1952, I just remember nodding off and I thought, "If I get caught I'll get fired." I kept trying to do things to keep awake. You could smoke at your desk back then, so I'd smoke to try to keep awake. There was no explanation. I hadn't been out the night before. I wasn't a party person. I'd never had a problem through high school.

But life went on. I got married and had seven children. And the problem continued. Doctors I saw about it attributed it to my pregnancies. I kept saying, "This isn't normal." I can remember falling asleep feeding one of my kids in a high chair. I used to fall asleep in checkout lines in the grocery store. People at work would tell new people, "If you notice Pat nodding off, just hit her." It was a big joke.

I always read the "Ann Landers" column. I always liked what she had to say. Every once in a while I'd disagree, but she put a lot of work into her answers. I was always surprised at how much investigating she did. It wasn't off the top of her head. She consulted experts.

One day in 1985, I was reading the column and there was one letter in it from a woman and I thought, "That's me! I could have written this!" She wrote that she had sleep episodes and her doctors told her she was working too hard. I thought, "There's someone else in the world!"

Ann Landers's reply was that it sounded like the woman had narcolepsy; I'd never heard the word before. She briefly explained it and talked about The Center for Narcolepsy in California. I called a friend and read the column to her. She said, "That's you!" And I said, "I can't believe I have to find out from Ann Landers what's wrong with me when my family doctors don't have a clue."

I wrote a letter to the Center for Narcolepsy. I got a personal letter back, not a form letter. It had a lot of clippings about the center and a list of doctors in the Chicago area that would diagnose or treat narcolepsy. So I went for an examination and was told I was a classic narcoleptic. And I thought, "Thank God." What had scared me most about my problem was what might happen if I was driving: the terrifying thought of getting in an accident and hurting or killing someone because I fell asleep at the wheel.

I'm fine now. I'm part of an adult synchronized ice skating team. Pretty good for a gal in her sixties. But I'm sorry to say I never wrote to thank Ann Landers. I often think about reading the letter about narcolepsy in her column and thinking, "If she didn't do what she did, God only knows when I would have found out what was wrong with me." She certainly changed my life.

Donna Lee Delk

WIFE/MOTHER/HOT-LINE VOLUNTEER

Portland

I only wrote to Ann Landers twice. The first time was when I was a teenager and was contemplating suicide. The second time was when I was in my thirties after I had gone back to college to earn a degree; I wrote to her then to share my ideas about what were suitable treats for grandchildren.

She never printed either letter but that didn't matter. Whenever I felt like I was in a life crisis, I knew I could write to her. It was like having a friend in the middle of the night. When you can't sleep, you write a letter, get it off your chest. Then it's done and you go to sleep.

I was raised by my widowed father. So I felt a lot was missing, the "how-tos": how to set a table properly, how to introduce people, what's the proper etiquette in gift giving for specific occasions. I felt like a bull in a china closet many times. I had many emotional problems. I needed a tender, loving mom for advice. That's what Ann Landers was to me.

I don't remember when I first saw the "Ann Landers" column. I was a teenager. It was probably an assignment for school. I fell in love with the column and it helped me every day because a normal day never felt normal. It consisted of me getting breakfast for my younger brother, getting both of us off to school, then coming home, doing laundry, housework, cooking, cleaning, helping my brother with his homework, and then doing my own. My father, a fireman, worked twenty-four hours on and forty-eight hours off, and then his first night off he'd go out with friends. So I was the one at home. I felt very isolated in this man's world and had a lot to confide, but really no one to confide in except Ann Landers. I was the one holding up the family and she was helping me.

About fifteen years ago she wrote about bad therapists, mentioning several red flags that patients should look for if they thought something wasn't right. At the time I was seeing a marriage counselor who was also a facilitator for a group therapy session my ex-husband and I were in. One night the group had a potluck at another patient's house. At this potluck we were hot tubbing and the therapist happened to sit next to me and touched my leg with his leg.

This made me very uncomfortable and made me realize that some other possibly inappropriate things were happening in the marriage counseling sessions. I reread Ann's column, and out of the seven or eight red flags mentioned, I noticed all of them. I contacted my personal therapist, whom I'd been seeing on and off for twenty-five years. I told her what I had discovered in Ann's column and she immediately contacted the marriage therapist as well as the ethics board. It was a good thing! I had recommended this marriage counselor to another couple and the wife told me that one day when she was at work, the therapist came in and kissed her on the cheek. But she had been too embarrassed to tell anyone. Ann saved us both.

I used to read her column every day! Or tried to, without fail. She had a sparkle in her eye, a spring in her step, a wit that is unmatched. She lived life. She knew people with the answers, if she didn't know something herself. She went through a divorce. She was human. She was a twin. A woman. A Jewish woman. She had a great uncanny way of relating and being there for a person. And she never ran out of gas!

I have worked on and off at hot lines since 1971, helping people in need as much as possible. I don't have the energy I used to, but Ann still inspires me—every day. I keep a picture of her in a frame in the living room.

Sometimes when my husband was leaving for work and I knew I wouldn't have time to read the whole paper, I'd tell him to go ahead and take it to work. But I'd tell him to bring the paper back home for me. He would always ask, "Why?" and I would say, "For Ann Landers," and he would laugh and say, "You never read the whole paper."

For me Ann Landers was the whole paper.

· LOT 2711 ·

A Complete Run of the Ann Landers Column

The *Sun-Times* edition of Sunday, October 16, 1955, was delivered to buildings and newsstands across Chicago in the darkness before dawn, its pages filled with such headlines as "Rails, Union agree on pay, avert strike," "Humphrey flies to see Ike," and "Plane crash in air: two killed here." But nothing in that day's paper was as interesting to Eppie as what appeared on page 52: her first column as Ann Landers.

It was twelve paragraphs and 709 words, topped by a "Your

Problems" logo and, as it would be for some time, highlighted by a whimsical cartoon illustrating the problem outlined in one of the lighthearted rather than serious letters in the column.

It's impossible to know what sort of impact those words had. Newspaper readers are creatures of habit. It takes a new column, a new voice, some time to work its way into that distinctive series of stops that make up each reader's path through a paper. And though there is no doubt that the "Ann Landers" column already had its share of regular readers—of the *Sun-Times* and the handful of other papers in which the column ran—it's impossible to know if any of them immediately noticed a change in the column's voice on that October morning. Eppie's voice was snappy from the start, as illustrated by her reply to the first letter published in her column.

"Dear Mrs. Landers: I've always regarded most marital mix-ups as very humorous—until now, that is, when the noose is tightening around my own neck. We have been married ten years and have two sons. I like auto racing, but my wife has no interest in it, so I've always gone without her. I've fallen in love with a woman with three children who is also very fond of auto racing. Her husband is ignorant and impossible. This may sound corny, but I think she would be a wonderful companion for me. I suppose you think I'm a louse—but I am stumped. I would like to have your advice on this problem.—Mr. K"

"Time wounds all heels—and you'll get yours," she responded, freshening up a line that was dusty even when used years before by Groucho Marx, but firmly conveying the message that this frolic was headed for disaster.

With Eppie's first stab at "Ann Landers" did someone

chuckle on the streetcar? Did someone read it to a friend over coffee, with some hey-you-gotta-listen-to-this enthusiasm? Did Mr. K., wherever he might have been, cringe or blush?

In retrospect, it is difficult to tell where Ruth Crowley's Ann Landers stopped and Eppie's began. It is obvious that in the first few months of writing the column, Eppie emulated Crowley. And why not? The voice in Crowley's "Ann Landers" columns was vastly different, and livelier, than that of the prim "lovelorn" columnists of the previous generation. In 1954 Crowley answered one person who criticized her column with a "Look, Bub, why don't you read the comics? There's no law that requires you to read what I write."

And in the weeks before Eppie started to write it, the "Ann Landers" column tried to counsel a teenage girl whose boyfriend was preoccupied with working on his car ("I can think of lots worse rivals than a car, baby"); a woman wanting to know how best to break up with her boyfriend ("Never mind the feelings. Just make sure you don't bruise the ego!"); a teenager jealous of his girlfriend's summer vacation flirtation ("Women! Aren't they a pain? [Sometimes]. But speaking as a woman, Buster, I'll clue you in . . . never let her know that you're jealous!").

Larry Fanning obviously played a role in the editing of Crowley's "Ann Landers" columns and was probably writing many of them during the time between Crowley's death and Eppie's hiring, along with the help of some women already affiliated with the newspaper. But he had inherited Crowley, who was certainly set in her writing style, methods, and language. In Eppie he had a pupil eager for his blue pencil and newspaper savvy. As he would later tell an interviewer, "[Eppie] isn't a psychiatrist. She isn't an intellectual, but she has a kind of wisdom about her, and I don't know where she got it."

But he knew what to do with it. Like a baseball scout who discovers a high schooler who can throw a fastball one hundred miles an hour, Fanning took Eppie's wisdom and taught her how to throw journalistic curves and sliders and change-ups, not to mention how to deliver brushbacks. They came in the form of learning which letters to choose for her column and how to make a satisfactory and interesting daily mix; cultivating the habit of addressing correspondents with such aggressively familiar terms as "Honey" and "Buster"; and developing her innate and catchy way with words, allowing her to express her morality and common sense in print. During the early years of the column, she told a teenager who wrote in asking about petting, "A lemon squeezed too many times is considered garbage." To the letter writer who criticized an earlier response by writing, "I feel better now that I have given you a piece of my mind," Eppie wrote, "I hate to take the last piece, but thank you for your letter."

The collaboration between Eppie and Fanning was fruitful, but it was also demanding, especially at the outset, often entailing work at the Lederers' apartment. Eppie called Fanning "Lair Bear"; Jules referred to him, in what was perhaps an unintended double entendre, as "the fan." He would often come to the Lederers' apartment for dinner and a few drinks and then work with Eppie on the column.

There is no doubt that Fanning molded Eppie and made her better faster than a less-inspired, tireless, and talented editor might have. Their collaboration would continue for more than a decade, even after Fanning moved from the syndicate to the *Sun-Times,* where he would be editor from 1959 to 1962, and when he became executive editor of the *Chicago Daily News.* The *Daily News,* an afternoon paper, was under the same ownership as the *Sun-Times,* with which it shared a building on the banks of the Chicago River. Fanning's working relationship with Eppie ended in 1966 when he left the paper, divorced his second wife, Ginny, and married Kay Field, the widow of Marshall Field IV. The next year the couple bought the *Anchorage Daily News* in Alaska, where Fanning was editor and publisher. He suffered a fatal heart attack in the newspaper office in 1971.

Until her death, Eppie always gave credit to Fanning. Was it possible that she was in love with him, or he with her? Many thought so. If it was not romantic love it was certainly a mutual admiration society. There was not a speech that I heard her give during which she did not mention his name. "I was trained by one of the world's best editors—Larry Fanning," she would often say. "He knew how to bring out the best in people. Larry convinced me that I could actually help those troubled souls— that I could make a difference—and that's what motivated me to give it my best."

If Fanning was impressed by Eppie's commitment and resourcefulness, he must have been slightly concerned about how this midwestern housewife was going to handle the atmosphere and pace of a 1955 newsroom.

There may be no other city in America, or the world, in which the newspaper business has been more romanticized than in Chicago. That image was born and solidified in 1928 when two former newspapermen, Ben Hecht and Charles MacArthur, sat down and created *The Front Page*, a play that met with great success on Broadway, spawned a number of film versions, and etched firmly in people's minds the image of newspaper reporters as hard-drinking and hard-hearted swashbucklers with a healthy disregard for cops, politicians, most women, and all editors. The play's raffish and quick-witted characters, almost all of them based on real-life Chicago newspaper people, became the basis for durable stereotypes that would linger for decades. They also were, and remain for some, the models for many reporters' self-image, cultivated with great care and carefree manner in newsrooms across the country.

Eppie was immediately smitten, later telling me, "What great characters there were in those days. It was a hard business not to fall in love with." And this, even though the newsroom was loud and chaotic, desks littered with papers, liquor bottles tucked in drawers, coffee stains and cigarette burns on the desks and floor, shouting and the occasional vulgar word or two. I was often in the *Sun-Times* office in these days, brought there by my father.

"Your father was one of the first people I met when I started at the *Sun-Times*. He was a great friend of Larry's," Eppie often reminded me. "He was a real newspaperman."

In 1955 my father, Herman, was forty-one and had spent his life in newspapers. His father had sold papers from a stand on the West Side of Chicago, and my father worked as the editor of his high school newspaper. He also worked as a police reporter for the City News Bureau while going to college at the University of Chicago; as rewrite man for the *Tribune;* as foreign correspondent when he was in the Marines serving in the

Pacific during World War II; as editorial writer, reporter, and editor at the *Sun;* and, when he met Eppie, as book and drama critic for the *Sun-Times.*

"They don't make them like your dad and Larry anymore," Eppie often said.

One thing accompanies every memory I have of the newsrooms of the 1950s. It is a sound, and if you have never heard it or it has been pushed from your brain by the soulless tapping of computer keys, the sound of typewriter keys banging is a beautiful noise. There is not a newspaper person of a certain age who does not feel this way. A typewriter's sound is able to instantly evoke the charming craziness that used to exist in newsrooms. It is the sound of effort, of work.

And there was Eppie in the middle of it all, arriving each day in her tailored suits, perhaps accented by a string of pearls, to find a desk piled with unopened mail. She had no office, no secretary, not even a phone. As my father would later recall: "A lot of the reporters and editors never thought she'd make it. She'd never really had a job before. But she was so friendly, outgoing, and full of questions. There's not a newspaperman alive who wouldn't want to sit with some good-looking dame and talk to her about his adventures in the business. It didn't take too long for her to be accepted and to feel right at home."

This might have allayed some of Fanning's worries. But he was obviously concerned about the ability of this tiny woman to shoulder the problems of a vast and diverse readership day after day. Eppie would often say, shaking her head, "When I started writing the column, I thought I was worldly and sophisticated, that I knew what life was about. I didn't know anything." Perhaps as a cautionary tale, Fanning gave Eppie a copy of Nathanael West's 1933 novel *Miss Lonelyhearts*.

The title character—never referred to as anything but Miss Lonelyhearts—is a twenty-six-year-old man who writes "an agony column" for a fictional paper named the *New York Post-Dispatch* in 1917. The novel is an allegory of America as it struggled through the depression, a tragicomedy of a man increasingly tormented by the suffering of the world.

At first Miss Lonelyhearts is amused by the work. But by the time we meet him, the despair-drenched letters are getting to him. There is the letter from "Desperate," who writes, "I am 16 years old and I don't know what to do. . . . I would like to have boy friends like the other girls and go out on Saturday nites, but no boy will take me because I was born without a nose—although I am a good dancer and have a nice shape and my father buys me pretty clothes. I sit and look at myself all day and cry. I have a big hole in the middle of my face that scares people even myself."

The endless pleas for comfort begin to seem alike, "stamped from the dough of suffering with a heart-shaped cookie knife." Miss Lonelyhearts becomes increasingly depressed by the letters and ever-tormented by his editor, Mr. Shrike, who tells him, "When they ask for bread don't give them crackers as does the church, and don't, like the state, tell them to eat cake. Explain that man cannot live by bread alone and give them stones." Miss Lonelyhearts tries to get himself fired by recommending suicide in his column. But Shrike tells him, "Remember, please, that your job is to increase the circulation of our paper. Suicide must defeat this purpose." Miss Lonelyhearts eventually makes a fatal mistake when he beats up a woman who had written to his column and is shot by her husband.

Eppie read the novel and once described it succinctly to a TV interviewer "This is a story about a man who was an advice columnist, and he let the problems get to him to the point where he couldn't function himself. I mean he really wigged out."

Whether Miss Lonelyhearts served as an example or not, Eppie certainly never "wigged out." In fact, she took to the column with remarkable confidence. Even during her first week as Ann Landers, she was self-assured and conversational and direct, her answers filled with the lively one-liners and direct responses that would ever characterize her work. Getting philosophical over dinner one night more than forty years after she started writing the column, Eppie told me: "I credit a lot of luck for everything I've done. I've always believed that success is the ability to use your luck. Some people don't even know when they get lucky. I did. Larry Fanning was good fortune smiling on me."

7

· LOT 1208B ·

Two Carved Owl Figures

The chance of having twins is one in about ninety births. It is not at all unusual for one of a pair of twins to become famous. Former NFL quarterback John Elway is a twin. Playwright Thornton Wilder was a twin. Painter Jackson Pollock was a twin, as is actor Kiefer Sutherland. Elvis was a twin. It is rare, however, for a set of twins to become notable or influential and so a persuasive case can be made that the most successful set of twins ever born were Esther Pauline and Pauline Esther Friedman.

When Eppie first started her column, the number of letters

was overwhelming. She felt that she needed help to make sure that every one of them, those backlogged and incoming, was answered. At the time, Eppie's identity as Ann Landers was known to only a small circle of editors, reporters, family, and friends. The column had always been written anonymously under the byline, and the paper wanted to keep it that way.

Twin sister Popo, of course, knew what Eppie was up to. Popo was then living in Hillsborough, a posh suburb thirty miles south of San Francisco. She and her family had moved there from Eau Claire in 1955, shortly after her husband, Mort, became president of his family's liquor distributorship. Popo would later tell a reporter, "After we settled in, I took stock of myself. I was a thirty-seven-year-old housewife with two teenagers, plenty of help in the house, and time on my hands. I was bursting with energy." Assistance from Popo seemed a perfect solution for Eppie, and she began, without Larry Fanning's knowledge, mailing stacks of letters to California.

Fanning was working tirelessly with Eppie, teaching her about the newspaper business, encouraging her to rely on outside experts, nurturing her wit and humor, and helping hone what would become Eppie's signature plain-talking style. Eppie would share Fanning's lessons with her twin, and Popo would answer the letters in accordance with Fanning's rules.

The arrangement between the twins seemed to be working well for the first few months. But when Fanning learned that Eppie had renewed the old "Campus Rat" partnership, he insisted the arrangement stop. In turn, Eppie demanded that if she was going to continue writing the column, she needed secretarial help. She was determined that every letter that arrived with a name and return address be answered, beginning a tradition that lasted until her death. She got want she wanted and was given not one but three assistants.

Eppie thanked Popo for her help and relieved her of her duties. But by that time Popo had been bitten by the advice bug and decided that the newspaper advice racket might be able to accommodate two Friedman sisters. She first approached the editor of the *San Mateo Times,* by some accounts offering to write an advice column for free, as a public service. The editors weren't interested. But those at the *San Francisco Chronicle,* whom she approached next, were. That paper was already running a syndicated advice column under the byline Molly Mayfield, but Popo impressed the bosses to whom she gave sample columns that she had written. Like her sister, she came with little experience, beyond coauthoring "Campus Rat" and the rhymed telegrams (shades of her sister's "Eppie-grams") that she often sent to friends and relatives. She signed them "Edgar Allan Popo."

For this potential new job, Popo had already come up with a byline: Abigail Van Buren, combining the names of a character from the Old Testament (". . . and David said to Abigail, blessed be thy advice") and that of the eighth president of the United States, which she deemed classy. The *Chronicle* editors decided to give Popo a shot and, elated, she called Eppie.

"She sounded disturbed," Popo would later tell a reporter. "I had been so happy over her success that I assumed she would be happy for me. But there was a long silence and finally she said, 'I guess it's all right if you don't get syndicated.'"

But syndicated is exactly what Popo got. The *Chronicle*

almost immediately dropped "Mayfield" and began running "Dear Abby" on January 9, 1956. Later that month, without telling Eppie, Popo signed a ten-year contract with the New York City–based McNaught Syndicate, and "Dear Abby" began appearing in papers around the country, including those in such large markets as New York, Houston, Dallas, and New Orleans.

This put a strain on the relationship between the twins, but it intrigued the media. The introduction of "Dear Abby" prompted a *Time* magazine story, the first of many national articles to be written about the columns. *Time* announced, "In her brief tenure on the job, the lovelorn writer, Mrs. Pauline Phillips, has proved herself just as snappy on the editorial draw as Ann Landers."

It is difficult in these first years of the twenty-first century, when advice—in columns, books, on radio and TV—is so widely available, to comprehend why two newspaper advice columns would be of such national interest. But in 1956, the columns were a sensation. What immediately set them apart from previous and other current advice columns was that the letters they published dealt with a wider and more intimate set of problems—issues that most readers had only whispered about but never before read about in a newspaper.

It was almost as if Americans—chafing under the tight collar of 1950s morality and conformity—had been awaiting a place where they could, under the comforting cloak of anonymity, air their troubles and frustrations; where they might find answers to questions they could not ask of relatives or bartenders or were reluctant to share with doctors or priests; or where they could merely eavesdrop on the collective malaise and peculiarities of others. The stream of letters began to flow from farm towns and high-rises, often beginning, "I never thought I would be writing to a newspaper but . . ."

And the answers the twins provided were refreshingly frank. Based on a foundation of common sense, the columns were alive with clever turns of phrase and comedic punch lines. Never hesitant to give letter writers a straight answer, Eppie and Popo had little tolerance for those who whined in print. "Turn off the waterworks, Mama, you're wasting natural resources," was a frequent Eppie response.

"From the start, her advice was breezy and crackled with one-liners," wrote David Grossvogel in his 1987 book, *Dear Ann Landers: Our Intimate and Changing Dialogue with America's Best-Loved Confidante.* The indefatigable Grossvogel was a Cornell University professor who spent four years reading every "Ann Landers" column published since 1955. His book was an attempt to analyze how the dialogue between Ann Landers and her readers reflected the changes in American society over three decades. He chose not to make comparisons between the "Ann Landers" and "Dear Abby" columns, but he did make a strong case that while "Dear Abby" tended toward the lighthearted and funny, "Ann Landers" had a taste for big issues, topics that had been previously taboo in "family newspapers."

Her very first published letter, from Mr. K, dealt with adultery, as did many others that first year and every year following. During the first years of the column she openly discussed such issues as venereal disease, virginity, and homosexuality, and all manner of other topics, both odd and compelling, but most novel to newspaper readers.

There was a letter from a person who believed she was

intercepting secret messages between Russia and Red China through her dental bridgework. There were letters from men complaining of wives who did not like sex ("She's a chunk of ice—just plain cold"). There was a letter from a wife whose husband spent his honeymoon night on the phone with his mother "trying to get her to stop crying"; from a father whose six-year-old son was a thief; from a woman whose daughter couldn't get a date; and from a teenager who had two problems, "my mother and my father. They are driving me nuts. They don't realize that I am a grown woman of fifteen."

These sorts of letters, combined with Eppie's sassy and practical responses, made the column all but irresistible to readers. A *Sun-Times* survey in the late 1950s noted that 85 percent of its female readers read "Ann Landers." More surprisingly, 45 percent of the male readers were also making the column a daily habit.

Chicago journalist John Callaway was working for the City News Bureau in 1956. This rough-and-tumble training ground for reporters was a place in which most tried hard to cultivate the hard-boiled *Front Page* image, where an admission of reading "lovelorn" columns would have been worse than admitting a fondness for milk over bourbon. But during a TV interview two decades later, Callaway told Eppie, "When I was copy boy [at City News] we used to sit around and read your column and argue about it." The same thing was happening at factories and across breakfast tables, at beauty parlors and in bowling alleys.

But if the nation's interest was considerably piqued by the content of the "Ann Landers" and "Dear Abby" columns, it rose to a level of fascination when it was revealed that the women who wrote the columns were twins.

In March 1956, less than six months after assuming the role of Ann Landers, Eppie was offered a one-year contract by the *Sun-Times* and its syndicate. That gave her the confidence to argue with Fanning and other editors that she be allowed to remove the column's cloak of anonymity. The perfect vehicle for doing so presented itself with an invitation for her to appear as a contestant on the TV show *What's My Line?* Millions of viewers got a look at her. Ann Landers finally had a face, and it was one with which the public would become increasingly familiar. With Fanning's prodding, Eppie began to accept invitations to make speeches in towns in which her column was carried and to foster relationships with editors so that she could lobby for better placement for her column and insist that photos of her run with it.

The rivalry with Popo was good for business. Such was the level of interest in this new breed of advice columnists that in 1958 *Life* magazine, then the biggest-circulation weekly in the country, deemed the twins ready for a profile. The headline loudly announced, "Twin Lovelorn Advisers Torn Asunder by Success." Though the sisters would later say that the story was filled with "misquotes," it would cement the image of a fiercely competitive and troubled relationship that would haunt them for a lifetime.

In the story, writer Paul O'Neill observed: "From the fierce rivalry between them . . . it sometimes appears that they are using U.S. journalism as a personal battlefield and its hundreds of newspapers as personal artillery in what appears to be the most feverish female feud since Elizabeth sent Mary Queen of Scots to the chopping block. It is a curious struggle. Each woman obviously considers her sister the most important human in the world. Each seems attracted as well as repelled by her twin. But neither seems able to stay a relentless hunger for dominance over the other, and each presses the thorns of minute but rankling grievances to herself as she engages in journalistic war."

However chilly the relationship between Eppie and Popo might have become by the time O'Neill was researching and writing his story, its appearance sparked the first public feud between the sisters and initiated an estrangement that would last, by some accounts, six years.

In the story, Popo said: "I understand why she's disturbed. She wanted to be the first violin in the school orchestra, but I was. She swore she'd marry a millionaire, but I did. I'm not trying to be the champion. It's just like playing poker. If you don't have to win, you gets the cards, and she's always just had to win. But I love her."

Eppie responded by saying, "That's her fantasy. She's just like a kid who beats a dog until somebody looks and then starts petting it."

However hurtful these comments may have been to Eppie and Popo, they surely brought smiles to the people running the organizations syndicating the rival columns. "Toting up the score at any given moment is a task calculated to drive any self-appointed umpire to heroin," O'Neill wrote. "Both syndicates . . . engage in all sorts of accusations and counter accusations." The *Sun-Times* published a brochure listing 180 papers that were running "Ann Landers," adding 15 more by the time O'Neill's story was being written. The "Dear Abby" team countered with the assertion that the column was running in more than 200 newspapers.

Each sister was in essence helping to sell the other's column.

During an era when most major cities had two or more daily newspapers, when one city's paper purchased one of the twins' columns, its rival in town was virtually forced to buy the other to match reader interest. They buried the competition, such as it was—"Dorothy Dix," then written by Muriel Agnelli, and a column written by Mary Haworth—and were ferocious in promoting their columns.

"Both constantly call, write and visit editors and publishers," wrote O'Neill. "Neither ever forgets a name and in two years they have accumulated a stupefying knowledge of the circulation, attitudes and problems of hundreds of U.S. newspapers. Both are uninhibited public speakers and whirl around the country appearing on radio and television and—dressed like visiting movie actresses—holding thousands of housewives spellbound in speeches at theaters and auditoriums."

As a vivid example of Eppie's desire to tackle big issues, she convinced the *Sun-Times* bosses to send her to Russia for three weeks in 1959. She studied Russian before the trip, and once in Moscow, in the company of an official Intourist guide, acted the role of foreign correspondent, interviewing strangers on the street, from kids to university students, and visiting courtrooms and factories. Though the Intourist factotum told Eppie that Russians were "too busy and hardworking to have problems," Eppie found people "tense and troubled," writing in the *Sun-Times* that "the problems of people are the same the world over . . . Ivan is worried about Irene's supervisor at the factory . . . Trina is concerned about her husband's drinking . . . Igor hates his mother-in-law."

The trip resulted in a twelve-part series that increased

Eppie's prominence and credibility as a journalist (though she would ever be loath to use that word to describe herself) and underscored the notion that she and her column were more "serious" than her sister and hers.

That year Eppie received more than a thousand invitations to speak to various groups and accepted more than one hundred of them, traveling to forty-some cities, reading letters in the backs of cars and limousines, sending her responses back to the *Sun-Times,* where her popularity had manifested itself in a staff of eight women to help with the mail.

Each of the twins was by then receiving ten thousand letters a week. In creating and cultivating their "Dear Abby" and "Ann Landers" columns and personas, the twin sisters from Sioux City were on their way to becoming the most successful newspaper columnists in history. But at what cost? Though in later years, after making peace and having other feuds, Popo would say, "I think being a twin is marvelous." Eppie more bluntly would say, "It's not easy being a twin."

· LOT 2999 ·

Annotated Manuscript
"Teenagers and Sex"

If the 1950s had been an enormous time of change for Eppie and her family, the 1960s would prove to be so for the entire planet. What a frustrating, complicated, confounding decade, the 1960s, a ten-year span that moved so quickly from relative innocence to what some considered insanity. And Eppie was at its epicenter, in daily conversation with millions of confused parents and teenagers—trying at once to keep up and stay ahead, to be true to herself and to what she knew; to reflect, from the thousands of letters she was getting every week, what was the American consensus on the issues of the day.

By 1961, the "Ann Landers" column was syndicated in 450 papers, with a readership of roughly 30 million. Very confident in the daily column she was producing, Eppie set out on a new challenge, to publish a book. Titled *Since You Asked Me,* it was a lively combination of previously published letters mixed with much of Eppie's philosophy and wisdom. Many of the topics discussed in this early book would be subjects she would continue to address for the next forty-one years: sex, choosing a mate, the relationship between parents and children, marital troubles, health, and aging.

As the nation would become better informed, and as times and attitudes changed, so did Eppie. Each decade would witness her doing an about-face on a number of issues. To her credit, she would always own up to and often explain her changes of heart or mind. There were, however, a handful of issues that Eppie remained relatively steadfast about throughout her career. Her attitudes on some of those topics—alcoholism, tobacco, teenagers and sex, and the role of sex in marriage—were clearly put forward in *Since You Asked Me.*

One of Eppie's most interestingly open-minded beliefs, given the comparative innocence of that time, concerned sexual relations between husbands and wives. In *Since You Asked Me,* Eppie wrote, "Do you know what the majority of women write about? They want to know what is 'respectable' in married love. 'Are there any moral limits?' they ask. I have consulted with clergymen of all faiths, physicians, psychiatrists and psychologists. They all agree that there is nothing indecent or unnatural in married love, provided it is agreeable to both parties and provided there are no harmful or painful effects. Sexual activity is the most private and intimate of all human relationships. It is the language of love. Married couples should feel free to express themselves as they please." This was a belief that Eppie held to firmly, even as the 1960s and 1970s unfolded, and some sexual scenarios became more complicated and "far out."

Perhaps the most compelling chapter in the book, because it seems to speak directly to what was happening in Eppie's personal life, was entitled "Double Trouble." This essay, devoted entirely to raising twins, began, "This should not be a chapter. It should be a volume." By 1961, Eppie and Popo had been officially on the outs for three years. Reportedly they did not even speak to each other during that time, preferring perhaps to let their rival syndicates do the public squabbling and arguing over which of their two columns was the most popular. In "Double Trouble," Eppie advised parents: "The most important thing to keep in mind is this: treat twins as separate and distinct personalities. Remember that each is a person. Each has an ego. Rear them as individuals and not as a single unit."

Eppie went so far as to outline a set of rules for raising twins:

Rule One: Do not dress them alike.

Rule Two: Separate your twins in school, if possible.

Rule Three: Encourage twins to follow separate interests and develop their individual talents.

Rule Four: Separate fields of endeavor will avoid head-on clashes or—worse yet—below-the-surface hostilities.

Rule Five: Do not compare one twin with the other and do not permit friends and relatives to do it.

Rule Six: Encourage your twins to be honest and open about their feelings.

Rule Four and its attending comments were almost poignant, since they seemed addressed directly to Popo. Eppie wrote: "In my opinion, twins should not compete in the same field. Such competition may produce a champion, but it is far more important to produce two healthy personalities."

If her relationship with Popo was troublesome, the rest of Eppie's personal life was almost blissful. As she was becoming world famous, Jules, too, had been doing well. Ever supportive of his wife in her career, he soon started to bridle at the limitations of being president of a company that made pens and pencils. He was eager for more and began investigating and investing in deals that might satisfy his ambitions. Some—including a plan to purchase a ball-bearing factory in Puerto Rico—didn't pan out. But one did.

In 1958, Jules was in Los Angeles, where he dropped in to visit a cousin of Eppie's, Morrie Mirkin, who was running a fledgling business, renting some four dozen used cars primarily to the soldiers stationed in nearby San Pedro and Long Beach.

Business was solid but Mirkin was eager to expand and he asked Jules for advice. He told Mirkin that he loved the company's name—Budget Rent A Car—but counseled that some people would simply not rent used cars. Jules offered to finance the purchase of a fleet of new cars in exchange for a stock option. He also set a price for the rentals, $5 a day and 5 cents a mile, half of what was being charged at the time by the leading car-rental companies, Hertz and Avis, and suggested that they begin selling franchises in other cities.

By 1960, Jules had resigned from Autopoint, bought out Mirkin's share of the business, and was on his way to becoming rich. But he was also extraordinarily busy and often away from Chicago, traveling across the United States and to Europe, Mexico, and South America to oversee expansion.

Young Margo was also active. She had been attending Brandeis University but left a few hours shy of a degree in February 1962 to plan a May wedding to a Boston hotelier named John Coleman. Though Eppie and Jules did not totally approve of the marriage—they simply didn't like Coleman—they eventually supported Margo's decision and threw a lavish ceremony at Chicago's Ambassador West Hotel with two rabbis, sixteen hundred azalea plants, an orchestra, and three hundred and fifty guests.

Though Margo's teenage years were behind her, Eppie would always feel a special connection to teens. And during her early years as Ann Landers, she felt a special obligation to them too, realizing that her column was one of the few places where they could hear a levelheaded dialogue about sex. She had been publishing a popular series of pamphlets for teenagers about the subject, but by 1963, she decided the issue deserved a book, in which she would explain: "For too many years the subject of sex among teenagers was soft-pedaled. There was a widely held theory that frank discussion might excite undue curiosity. 'Don't give the kids ideas' is the way it was put. Well, the kids already have ideas, and many of them have put the ideas into practice. Adult silence serves only to widen the gap between two generations which are already too far apart. I am a strong advocate of open discussion—and the more open the better."

The book, *Ann Landers Talks to Teen-Agers About Sex,* devoted chapters to such topics as going steady, sex, and alcohol. More than 30 percent of the "Ann Landers" letters were coming from teens, indicating that they trusted her and were willing to accept her as an authority, and as someone who could guide them through their problems. Her ability to connect with teenagers was reflected in letter after letter: "I am a high school senior who will be 18 in four months. I read your column every day and I think you dig teenagers"; "I am writing to you because I can't talk to my folks about this problem"; "I'm worried to death and can't talk to anyone else . . . I think I'm pregnant."

For teens of the 1960s Eppie functioned as teacher, counselor, and nonjudgmental friend, roles that others in their lives were unable or unwilling to fulfill. By so doing, she not only endeared herself to the generation that would become her most loyal readers, but she became for some of them the mother they didn't have, as many letter writers would touchingly tell her.

"Dear Ann Landers:

"I am writing about the lady whose husband ignored their son because he had a physical deformity. I am a fifteen-year-old boy and my father ignored me for as long as I can remember. I don't know why. I was a normal, healthy baby, and I was never any trouble.

"I was always close to my mother. She took me nearly every place she went. I'm sure she did this to make up for my father who didn't pay any attention to me. I spent so much time with my mother that I never learned to do things boys usually do, like play ball or wrestle or swim. I guess you might say I was a sissy.

"Shortly after my ninth birthday, my mother died. Since then I've felt like an orphan. I have a hard time in school. I guess I need someone to be strict with me and tell me how far to go. My dad never sets any limits. He just ignores me and I do as I please.

"The kid next door has a father who is very strict. I envy him even though he complains all the time that he can't do anything on account of his old man. He doesn't know how lucky he is.

"I don't know why I am writing to you except maybe to say you are sort of a substitute mother for me. I learn a lot from your column. Would you think it crazy if I told you that sometimes I dream you are my mother? I think I'll sign off before you decide I'm a complete nut. Thank you for everything —Johnny."

Perhaps it was letters like this—expressing the yearning for a long-lost loved one—or maybe it was the increasing uncertainty and craziness of the times, but in 1964, Eppie and Popo made efforts toward peace. They reconnected over the phone and arranged a trip with their husbands to Bermuda, in celebration of their twenty-fifth wedding anniversaries. There, Eppie would later tell a reporter, "We laughed. We had fun. And then the relationship, it was back to where it was before." And where it would remain for nearly two decades. The twins made a bargain on that trip to never discuss each other's work or each other's column with each other or, more important, with the mob of journalists always eager to interview them.

9

· LOT 2700 ·

Journal, Uniforms, Photographs, Film from 1967 Visit to Vietnam

A nn Landers wants to see you after her speech," John Graham whispered to me as I walked into the second-floor gymnasium/auditorium of the Latin School one morning in 1965. He was the headmaster, or principal, of the school. I was a freshman in high school. "She wants me to bring you over to her, so sit here so I'll know where you are."

He pointed to a chair and I sat, remembering that my father had told me early that morning, "I told Eppie—Ann Landers—to say 'Hello' to you when she speaks at the school today." He meant well, not realizing the potential embarrassment this might cause.

Details of Eppie's speech have faded over the years. But it would be impossible to forget the sound of her voice. It was something that did not seem to fit her body. It was not an elegant voice but rather rough-edged. The words came out as if pouring over marbles or rocks. And when she spoke (or when she smiled), her mouth curled up along the left side of her face, giving her a vaguely sinister look and reminding me (then and forever) of Jimmy Cagney in one of his gangster roles.

After her speech, Eppie was immediately surrounded by a circle of teachers and students, full of praise and asking for autographs. I was hoping Mr. Graham might have forgotten about fetching me, but I felt his hand on my arm and heard him say, "C'mon, let's go," and we elbowed our way through the crowd and finally to the tiny woman at its center.

"This is Rick Kogan," he said. Eppie took the hand I had extended, grabbed it in both of hers, and said, "You look just like your mother," not exactly the thing a freshman boy was eager to have broadcast in front of a pack of schoolmates. And I think I heard a couple of giggles as Eppie thanked the people gathered around her and said to me, "Will you take me out to my car?" It wasn't really a question. She grabbed my arm and as we walked down the stairs and out of the building, she said, "I hope I'm not embarrassing you. Your father said to say hello."

"No, it's . . . it's nice to meet you."

"You probably don't remember, but we've met before. You were much younger. You know I just love your father. Now, tell me, what's your favorite subject?"

"English, I guess."

"Maybe you'll become a writer."

I don't remember much of the rest of the conversation, but I do know I felt awkward and Eppie was inquisitive, and the faces of many of my classmates were pressed against the second-floor windows, obviously wondering what the hell I was doing having a private conversation on the sidewalk with Ann Landers. I do remember her asking, because it was the first time any adult had ever asked me such a question, "Are you staying away from drugs?" and my saying "Uh, yes," as, to my great relief, she began to get into her limousine. "Don't let friends make you do anything you don't want to do," she advised.

I watched the car head west on Scott Street and within seconds—in what would many years later become a familiar scenario whenever people saw me in Eppie's company or learned that Ann Landers and I were friends—I was peppered with questions.

"What makes you such a big deal?" asked one classmate.

"She works at the same paper as my dad," I said.

"You think she really believes some of that stuff she said?" asked another.

"I don't know," I said.

"Did she give you any advice?" asked a senior girl.

"She told me not to get high," I said.

That hardly made me a member of an exclusive club. Eppie was saying the same thing to anyone who was reading her column. Only a couple of years before, when Eppie wrote *Ann Landers Talks to Teen-Agers About Sex,* there was no mention in it of marijuana, long hair, free love, flower power, or some of the other diversions and lifestyles that were starting to define the counter-culture. Drugs had been mentioned in the column almost from its outset, at first masquerading under such euphemisms as "stay awake pills" or "Bennies." But by the time she spoke at my high school, marijuana was a frequent topic of the column's letters, and Eppie consistently cited experts in advising readers that marijuana "is a dangerous way to get kicks" and "a gutless approach to liv-ing." In another, more pragmatic response, she warned readers against drug use because "we do not yet know the effects it may produce over a period of several years."

Eppie was beginning to take a stand in print on many con-troversial issues. That was okay by John Trezevant, the man who had taken over editing her column from Larry Fanning, but he didn't want her getting into political matters. "Her poli-cies and replies are her own," Trezevant, executive vice presi-dent of the *Sun-Times* and *Daily News,* told a magazine reporter. "Though I urge her to stay out of such things as political endorse-ments of candidates or pending legislation. But Eppie's been able to break most of the accepted rules and do things the way she wants by sheer force of personality."

Initially, Eppie took Trezevant's advice, avoiding any contro-versial issues relating to politics. But her column was increas-ingly becoming a forum for the social issues of the times. Homosexuality was a particular hot-button issue. It was in her column in 1956, its first year, that the word *homosexual* was ever printed in U.S. newspapers. So incendiary and taboo was it that the publisher of the paper in St. Joseph, Michigan, refused to print the column in which the word appeared, telling Eppie, when she called him to ask why, that he did not think the subject was fit for a "family newspaper." He said he was going to run a column on page one explaining his decision. "I was in a rage," she later told me. "I called this man up and said that homosexuality was a human problem and that is what my column deals with. He wouldn't budge, so I explained how many of his readers would buy other papers to see what he wasn't printing. Well, that convinced him, and I never had another problem with that man."

Eppie would continue for more than three decades to regard homosexuality as an aberrant behavior problem caused by "arrested development. This in a very real sense is a dysfunction, or an illness" even after the American Psychiatric Association removed the word *sick* from its definition describing homosexuals. She was, however, steadfast in urging readers to be tolerant of the homosexual lifestyle and homosexuals. But more important, she allowed her column to become a forum for debate and information on the subject.

Her antigun stance also appeared early, further fueled by the assassinations of John F. Kennedy, Martin Luther King, Jr., and her friend Robert Kennedy. She loved Alcoholics Anonymous. By the 1960s, most readers were familiar with many of her attitudes. They had gotten to know this Ann Landers person and felt increasingly comfortable in conversation with her or just eavesdropping on the chat she was having with America.

For all of her imprint advocacy, she understood, too, that not all her readers were coming to her column for a series of discussions of controversial issues, but sometimes to escape them, to find in the papers' back pages some shelter from the storms raging in news headlines. "I wouldn't want to use three letters from teenagers in one day, or three sad letters or three funny letters," Eppie said. "Every day I want something in there that will educate people—a good piece of information that they probably could not get anyplace else. And I want it, every day, to contain some hope." And so she was adept at leavening serious topics with letters about such matters as hanky-panky at office parties, acne, table manners, and meddlesome in-laws.

Whenever she would venture into the topic of cooking, those columns elicited a volume of responses that did not seem commensurate with the subject's lack of gravity. She was buried in mail and advice in 1960 after admitting she was not very good at making gelatin desserts. And a later column became an even greater culinary crisis. It occurred after she published a recipe for meat loaf, courtesy of her older sister Dorothy. A typical letter read: "Dear Ann Landers: You should stick to advising people who have problems and not get into things you don't know anything about. . . . My wife has been making meat loaf for years and it has always turned out dandy. Since we were having guests for dinner, she decided to give Ann's recipe a try because she thought somehow it would be better than her own. Well, Ann Landers' meat loaf was a flop. Nobody said anything but there was plenty left over for the dog—Disappointed in Adrian, Michigan." Before the meat loaf "controversy" died down, some forty thousand readers had voiced their disgust. What a crowd, these readers. But Eppie learned from them and was ever grateful.

As the decade wore on, Eppie was feeling frustrated by having to keep some of her political opinions out of the column. In person she was an outspoken critic of the war in Vietnam. But she would not allow that voice, that opinion, to appear in print. She was engaged in what had to be a difficult juggling act. The name Ann Landers was owned by the syndicate, and thus Eppie often struggled to make the distinction between what was being said as Eppie Lederer and what was, or was not, being said, as Ann Landers. Eppie was more liberal on such matters as the war, equal rights for women, and abortion than she could allow the column to be.

Finally, Eppie felt she had to do something about the war. "Vietnam was a real mess," she told me. "I really felt for years that it was an immoral and impossible war. I was always telling Hubert Humphrey that, and in 1967 he said, 'Go there. Talk with some of the people one-on-one.' He thought I would come back convinced that the war was not only just but that the United States was going to win it."

So, in 1967, Eppie took a ten-day trip to Vietnam. She would later tell me that she visited twenty-five hundred men in hospitals there. She loved to relate one particular encounter, when a man limped toward her on crutches, saying, "I smell perfume. I haven't smelled perfume in a long time." He moved closer, eager for a hug. "Be careful," Eppie said. "I could be dangerous."

That was one of the few lighthearted moments in a trip that would be a personal watershed for Eppie, and a highly publicized one. On her return to Chicago, the *Sun-Times* hailed her as a "Miracle Worker," and one soldier was quoted saying: "Most celebrities who come here walk through a couple of wards, get their pictures taken, and leave. This woman has visited every single patient. It's almost eleven at night and I know she's been on her feet since this morning. Where in the world does that little woman get all her energy?"

Eppie came back convinced more than ever that the war was a bad thing, though it wasn't until 1972 that her antiwar views began to appear in her column. She quietly took hits from some critics, including in an editorial in the *New York Times,* who considered her trip a personal publicity stunt. What the *New York Times* did not know is that when she returned from Vietnam she carried with her hundreds of phone numbers scrawled on pieces of paper, numbers of family members and friends and lovers of the soldiers she had met.

"It took me weeks to call them all," she told me one afternoon, as she proudly showed me an album of photos taken during her Vietnam trip. "I had little notes with numbers and names. I called the soldiers' relatives and told them that I was saying hello from Roger or George or whatever the name of the solider was. They always asked how he was doing and I had to tell a lot of white lies. I didn't want them to hear from me that their son or husband had lost a leg or an eye. I usually said they had colds or something that wasn't very serious. They were so grateful and then we'd just talk about other things. Some of these people stayed in touch for years. Some became my friends for life just because of a phone call."

· LOT 2635 ·

Large Pair of Chinese Cinnabar
Lacquer Baluster Vases

O f all the things that filled Eppie's apartment, the most striking was a bust of John Fitzgerald Kennedy that sat in front of a window in a library just off the living room. It faced inward, away from the lake, and looked best at night, framed by the darkened window, looking as if it were a huge head suspended in the sky. The sculpture was by Salvador Dalí, one of his more realistic efforts. Jules had purchased the bust for $25,000 at an auction and given it to Eppie for her birthday in 1971. It fit nicely in the new apartment into which he and Eppie moved the following year. It was located on a one-block stretch of Oak Street called East Lake Shore Drive, half a block east of where they had lived since 1954. It was arguably the most prominent stretch of apartments in the city, anchored at its west end by the Drake Hotel, and made up of seven apartment buildings that flanked a small park and offered magnificent views north along the shore of Lake Michigan.

This was the apartment Eppie would live in until her death. (Indeed, she would die in the apartment.) She was always proud of the place and delighted to give first-time visitors "the tour." How much she liked people—or how comfortable she felt with them—would often dictate how many of the fourteen rooms she would show them. For me and many other visitors, the JFK bust was the apartment's most dramatic element, its hair fashioned from clay cleverly mixed with paper clips that gave it a kinetic quality, as if the hair was being blown by some unseen breeze.

Eppie had met JFK in the Oval Office when he was president and she was chair of the Christmas Seals campaign against tuberculosis. As she told *New Yorker* writer Christopher Buckley more than forty years later, Kennedy "was so attractive. A knockout. Sex appeal oozed from every pore. He was the womanizer from Hell. I mean, this guy had women all over the place. In the swimming pool, the locker room. Of course, he had a bum back, for one thing, and the women had to do all the work."

She loved the JFK bust. And at the time it was given to her, she appeared to be madly in love with Jules, telling interviewers, "Jules is my best friend . . . He's always buying me presents. He loves to . . . My husband finds me fascinating . . . He thinks he's the luckiest man in the world."

By this point in her life and career, Eppie's circle of friends included many household names: columnist Art Buchwald and his wife, Ann; Walter and Betsy Cronkite; Supreme Court Justice William O. Douglas; Senator Eugene McCarthy; and Barbara Walters, to name but a few. Many of these people, and other famous friends, valued Eppie's opinions—in print or in the many personal notes she sent—as much as did her readers. Edward Kennedy responded to one of her columns by writing her a personal note: "Your response to the very moving letter from a young girl seeking safety and comfort on her neighborhood street was very appropriate. The gun crisis is so serious. I hope to schedule hearings on the gun bill soon." And in response to what was certainly a personal bit of advice Eppie sent to him in 1975, then–U.S. secretary of defense Donald Rumsfeld wrote back: "Thank you for your very kind comments on my recent television appearance. In accordance with your advice I will try to avoid discussing Angola or whatever the popular military subject of the day may be."

In addition to the famous, Eppie's circle included a vast array of experts on all conceivable subjects. The use of experts had become a cardinal feature of her column: relying on doctors, sociologists, scientists, psychiatrists, politicians, and any other people notable in their fields to help answer questions from readers. It was a mutually beneficial arrangement. The column used the experts because they gave it the heft of authority; the experts received instant national recognition and the increased stature (and perhaps business) that resulted. Would anybody not take a phone call from Ann Landers?

"And every day was a learning experience for me," Eppie told a reporter, defining her job as "an opportunity to educate. I want to let people in trouble know that others have problems, too. I want to be the shoulder to cry on. Maybe I can't solve the problem, but at least I can turn on the light so they can see it."

She had become so adept and artful at mixing topics that the millions turning to her column each day never knew what to expect. One day they might find a letter from a woman complaining, "Stop criticizing women who undress in the closet. . . . For three years I was mauled, pinched, and even slugged. No matter what I was doing, regardless of my mood, my husband was after me, leering, panting, lusting, and grabbing. Finally, I couldn't stand the sight of him." On another day this: "I'll make it quick. I know you're busy. He is a physical culture nut. Loves to walk everywhere. Picks dinner places miles away and insists we walk back to burn up the calories. I love him madly but my feet are killing me. What should I do?" On another day readers might find a listing of organizations that could help with drinking or gambling problems, or letters dealing with elderly parents or out-of-control teens. On another day they might find a sex quiz, or a question about etiquette, as in this letter from a woman wondering about what to wear to a funeral: "Could a veil like Jackie Kennedy's be worn with glasses, or should I get contact lenses? Are white gloves too dressy?"

Eppie also enjoyed reprinting "favorites" sent by readers, and one might find a checklist, short essay, or poem. And there were sometimes topics so wild and unexpected that they defied categorization, such as an investigation into the sleeping habits of cows, when one letter writer wondered if cows, who apparently sleep standing up, could really be "tipped" over.

Eppie's advice ("Tip the waitress, but leave the cows alone") relied on opinions from a curator at Chicago's Lincoln Park Zoo, the Department of Dairy Sciences at Iowa State University, a past president of the Nebraska State Dairy Association, and students in a fraternity house at the University of Wisconsin. Indeed, *was* there anybody who would not take a phone call from Ann Landers?

But for all her playfulness, Eppie was more committed than ever to tackling important, and often controversial, issues. In December 1971, she devoted her column to what she called at the time "the most feared word in the English language," *cancer*. The column came at the behest of her good friend, philanthropist Mary Woodard Lasker, a champion of medical research and urban beautification. With her husband, Albert Davis Lasker, a pioneer advertising executive, she established a legacy of effective philanthropy through her own efforts and her public support of important causes. Mrs. Lasker was one of the country's best-known and most effective advocates of increased public funding for medical research. She made the case for federal funding by warning, "If you think health is expensive, try disease!"

Eppie addressed the column to her readers and in it detailed not only some chilling statistics about cancer (of 200 million Americans alive, 50 million were likely to develop cancer) but illustrated how comparatively little was being spent on research (for every person in the country, the government was spending $125 on the war in Vietnam and $19 on foreign aid, but only 89 cents on cancer research). She asked her readers to write to their senators, urging them to support a $100 million cancer research bill pending before Congress.

"I happened to be in Washington a day or so after that

column," Barbara Walters recalled for *Biography*. "And do you know, I saw trucks arriving at the Senate. And I said, 'What are all those trucks?' And they said, 'They're mail trucks. Ann Landers put in something and told them to write their senators.' And this is what happened. Eppie has power."

A blizzard of mail, variously estimated at between three hundred thousand and 1 million cards and letters, from "Ann Landers." readers hit Washington. Capitol Hill had never seen anything like it. No politician could afford to ignore that kind of pressure. Eppie was invited to be present on December 23, 1971, when President Richard Nixon signed the National Cancer Act.

It was as if Eppie had her finger on the popular pulse, and her column did not simply reflect but gave voice to national concerns and issues. By the mid-1970s, she backed a woman's right to have an abortion, discouraged adopted children from tracking down their biological parents who did not wish to be found, and suggested that suicide, for terminally ill patients, should not be universally condemned. Her opinions were so influential that even some that were too political for her column made it into print. For example, in April 1974 she believed that for the good of the country Nixon should resign as president because of the Watergate scandal. She suggested this during a speech at Notre Dame University and made national headlines.

Her letters continued to reflect the rapidly changing times. "There have been so many changes in the last ten years and more in the last twenty-five than in the previous two hundred," she told a *New York Times* reporter in 1974. "There was a time when I thought that no unmarried girl, no matter how old, should have any physical relations with a man. Well, I see now that is not the brightest approach. Some girls can handle sex outside marriage if they're sufficiently mature . . . an awfully smart nineteen or a darn steady stable twenty. But I firmly believe that high school girls should stay intact."

Her readers were, by this time, also well aware of how she felt about certain issues that had not changed. She so hated smoking that she might have been the first to make public the dangers of secondhand smoke when she cited a report from the Interstate Commerce Commission, which stated, "Second hand smoke is an extreme irritant to humans. . . . Non-smokers can inhale smoke equivalent to one pack if they spend a day in a smoke-filled room." She was so pro–gun control that she had begun referring to firearms owners as "gun nuts" and prompted the National Rifle Association to issue a statement: "She knows nothing about existing gun laws and apparently prefers it that way."

Her readers, and there were an estimated 60 million of them in the 810 papers that carried her column during the 1970s, might not have agreed with everything that appeared in the column, but they were loyal and Eppie understood that. In her 1975 book, *Ann Landers Speaks Out,* Eppie wrote: "Hundreds of people write every week because they are lonely. They just need to talk to someone. I'm the shoulder to cry on. The unseen face. They can tell me their side of the story and I won't yell at them, or question their veracity, or tell them they're crazy. . . . I am at once flattered and surprised when professional writers ask how I get through to people. They say, 'You seem to have a direct line to the masses, to the average American.' But I have never met a mass and I have yet to meet anyone who will admit he is average. I address myself to individuals, not masses. People who suffer, suffer alone."

In some ways, however, Eppie seemed to be above suffering. Indeed, her life appeared to be perfect. As she told a *New York Times* writer in 1975, "I have been very lucky. I have good health, amazing vitality, good head, good body, wonderful husband and daughter." But in *Ann Landers Speaks Out,* Eppie wrote this: "I've come to understand that many people, who appear to be in complete control, calm, and self-assured, may be full of doubts, and loaded with anxieties. God alone knows the masks people wear, the brave fronts they put up—the Academy-Award–winning performances that go on every day, all around us."

11

· LOT 2704 ·

Correspondence to Ann Landers
Regarding Her Divorce

Being a divorced woman—or a divorcée, to use an old-fashioned word—was hardly something that would have raised eyebrows in the mid-1970s. The country had undergone something of a "divorce revolution" in the prior two decades, as a result of a significant cultural shift in ideas regarding marriage, gender roles, and, a particular ideal of the '60s—the right of each individual to pursue health and happiness. In 1955 the divorce rate was about one in every four couples. By 1971, the ratio was one in three.

Indeed, even Eppie had changed what had once been a

rather strident attitude regarding divorce. During her first month as Ann Landers, she had received a letter from a man asking whether he should divorce his wife, whom he suspected of fooling around. Eppie responded, "Divorce is no solution. . . . Try to rekindle the old spark." Weeks later, in response to a wife writing to complain that she was contemplating divorce because she and her husband had nothing in common, Eppie wrote, "To me divorce is a dreadful thing."

She remained so rigidly opposed to divorce—except when a relationship was marked by physical abuse—that one 1962 letter writer demanded, "How come your dateline isn't Vatican City?" But her attitude changed along with the country within the next decade.

If the notion of a divorce was hardly shocking in 1975, what did stun people was to learn that Ann Landers—the lady who solved the problems, not the lady who had them—was to be the one calling it quits. The news would come from Eppie herself in the form of a column that appeared on July 2, 1975, two days before her fifty-seventh birthday.

For all of her candor in public and print, Eppie rarely shared personal details of her life in the column. She broke that rule in 1973 when writing about the death of Jules's mother, Gustie Lederer, whose affectionate nickname for Eppie was "Eppeleh with the Keppeleh," Yiddish for "Little Eppie with the good head." Wrote Eppie tenderly, "For 34 years, we never exchanged one unpleasant word." Most loyal readers knew about the marriage between Eppie and Jules, even remembering the 1969 column she devoted to their thirtieth wedding anniversary. Eppie always referred to Jules as "my doll, my beautiful guy" and she inscribed the books she wrote and the linings of her fur coats, "Jules' wife."

It was a difficult decision for Eppie to make her divorce public. Some of those closest to her advised that she not address the divorce in the pages of the nation's newspapers, arguing that it might have a negative effect on her career. Even Eppie had concerns, later recalling, "[I feared] that my divorce might end my career. I thought that some of the editors or publishers would say, 'Well look, she can't keep her own marriage together, what is she doing telling other people how to keep theirs?'"

But in a typically gutsy move, Eppie decided that the news should come directly from her. And she was characteristically direct, telling her readers that she and Jules had split after thirty-six happy years of marriage. She asked in the column that her readers refrain from inquiring about the reasons behind the breakup. She was being up front, but this was still a very sensitive, and private, matter.

I vividly recall the buzz it caused. I was freelancing for the *Sun-Times* at the time and on the day the column appeared, the newsrooms of the *Sun-Times* and *Daily News,* which shared the fourth floor of the same building in downtown Chicago, were alive with chatter.

Not many reporters or editors were shocked by the content of the column. Divorce was no newsroom novelty. It was just that Eppie's life had somehow seemed above the everyday problems that afflicted to rest of us.

The conversations mostly centered on other, more newspaper-related matters, such as how the column's news might affect readership, and particularly how the column appeared in print. It did not fill its regular space, leaving a large chuck of blank space at its end. Eppie had requested that editors leave this space empty "in honor of a great marriage that didn't make it to the finish line."

"That really makes the column jump out at you," said one reporter.

"Yeah, but I wonder if this will hurt her in the long run," said another.

Such worries proved unfounded. Her bosses backed her. Emmett Dedmon, who headed Field Enterprises, which syndicated the column, said, "We don't think it will have any impact on the column. We regard it as a personal tragedy." And no papers dropped her column.

If the public was surprised to read about the couple's divorce, Eppie herself always maintained that she did not see the breakup of the marriage coming and was stunned when it happened. I believed Eppie when she said that. As practical as she was, she was also an idealist. She would have to be in order to survive in the advice business. She really did believe that human beings could weather almost any problem with professional help, courage, chutzpah, and faith. Idealists also believe in forevers—of a job, good health, marriage—even when realities begin to eat away at such a notion. And some might speculate that realities were doing damage to the Lederer marriage by the 1970s.

Both Eppie and Jules were extremely hardworking. The children of immigrant parents, both valued and were driven to success. Jules was an aggressive businessman and traveled often.

Eppie was, and would remain, utterly passionate about and committed to her work. At the time she and Jules decided to divorce, she was only three years away from being named "Most Influential Woman in America" by the *World Almanac*. Eppie was a dynamo, always in demand, and frequently the Lederers were on the road, rarely to the same place. She was sitting on some of the most prestigious boards in the country, including the Board of Overseers of Harvard Medical School, and in 1974 traveled to China for three weeks as part of an exchange sponsored by the American Medical Association.

When some people, even casual friends, learned of the split, they were not surprised. Those defending Jules argued that he had grown tired of Eppie's fast-paced lifestyle. Those lining up on Eppie's side suggested that Jules had grown envious of her fame or would have told you she simply had outgrown Jules.

Whatever the feelings of personal friends, the public reaction was, in one Eppie word, "remarkable." She received more than thirty thousand letters, virtually all of them supportive of or sympathetic to her decision. So moved was she that these would be the only letters from readers that she ever kept. And she kept them all.

"There was so much love," Eppie told a TV interviewer a few years later. "I felt such an outpouring of good feeling—'We're for you, don't quit writing,' 'Dentists get toothaches,' and 'Doctors get sick'—those kinds of things—'Don't feel you're a failure,' 'We know you. We love you. We're with you. And just keep doing what you're doing.' Thousands of letters like that and that was immensely supportive to me."

Though Eppie initially did not discuss the reasons for the

divorce, she was flattened by the split, seeking comfort from Margo, her sister Popo, Hesburgh, and other close friends. Thanks to them, and her readers, she was back on firm emotional ground when the divorce became official during a fifteen-minute session in a judge's chambers on October 17, 1975, twenty years and one day after her first column as Ann Landers had appeared in print. But if that irony caused Eppie to wonder whether becoming Ann Landers had contributed to the breakup of her marriage, she never said a word about it, instead insisting in a later interview with the *Chicago Sun-Times,* "My husband was very proud of my accomplishments. He had success of his own. Jules never thought of me as Ann Landers. I was always Eppie to him. At no time did Jules ever make me feel I wasn't giving him enough attention, or that Ann Landers was taking over Eppie Lederer." Eventually, however, Eppie would reveal what did end the marriage.

I had, over the years, read about the reasons for the divorce. Almost every interviewer, even decades later, asked about it. But over dinner one night I got the story firsthand. I had become her editor by this time, and we were out to dinner.

"How is everything at home?" Eppie asked. "How's your wife?"

"Not so good," I said. "I've moved out."

I was shocked that the words came so easily, almost like a confession. Very few people, not even some of my closest friends, knew about the problems with my marriage.

"What is it?" asked Eppie, looking concerned.

"It's just . . . ," I started to say, startled to feel my voice crack.

She reached across the table and grabbed my arm. "It's okay,

honey. Let me tell you how it was for me . . ." and Eppie pro-
ceeded to share the details of her split with Jules.

Apparently Jules had a girlfriend, a woman he was keeping
in an apartment in London, and the relationship had been going
on for some time. He finally told Margo about it and she
insisted that he tell Eppie.

"I was stunned, I mean shocked," Eppie said. "I didn't want
some kind of arrangement, so I said, 'The marriage is over.' I
don't think he believed me. I think he thought we could work
something out, but I gave him thirty days to move out."

She told me that just before he moved out, she bought him
two dozen pairs of brown socks, two dozen handkerchiefs, a
dozen shirts, and a dozen pairs of shorts; that she wrote down
the number of the doctor, the drugstore, and the dry-cleaning
store. "And I said, 'Good-bye, good luck,' " she said.

I just sat there listening, instead of peppering her with questions. I had the feeling that she was telling me the story of her
divorce not so much in order to provide me some sort of map—
the territories of the two relationships were vastly different—
but rather, as she so often did in her column on divorce and so
many other matters, to offer you're-not-alone-in-this comfort.

Jules would eventually marry the other woman, a nurse
named Elizabeth Morton who was twenty-eight years younger
than Jules. Eppie said that she was devasted at first, but in a
short time she decided that "hate and jealousy are no good for a
person. They will make you emotionally, physically exhausted."
She said she eventually "had warm feelings toward Jules."

His fortunes had started turning sour a few years before the
divorce. In 1968, Budget Rent A Car was purchased by San

Francisco–based Transamerica Corporation for roughly $10 million in stock, a large portion of which went to Jules. He also accepted a five-year contract to remain with the company as president. But Transamerica's stock took a beating in the early 1970s, and Jules, a born entrepreneur, never fit into the culture of a large corporation. When his contract was up, he was happy to walk away, confident he would be successful on his own. He tried to launch a European hamburger franchise. It failed. So did a health-care service deal. He was depressed and spending an increasing amount of time in the town house he and Eppie owned in London, the city where he met Elizabeth. "I think that when the Budget Rent A Car went sour, Jules really just lost his way," Eppie said.

I asked Eppie if she ever met Elizabeth. "No. I never wanted to," she said. "From everything I ever heard, she was a nice person, very soft spoken. It would have just killed me if he'd been taken in by a tramp."

My drink was empty by then, and Eppie motioned to the waiter and said, "You can bring him one more." Then she said to me, "So, tell me, what's going on?" and over the next hour I did, with an increasing sense of relief merely in being able to unload, not at all fearful of her being judgmental. Mostly she just nodded while she listened. Every once in a while she would ask, "And how does she feel about that?" After dinner, walking the half-block from the restaurant back to her apartment, she said, "Don't worry, honey. Divorce doesn't have to mean failure—you both have a chance to have new lives, better lives. But I think you both have to get out and get on with it."

I just nodded and hugged her in front of her building.

"Thanks," I said.

"If you need to talk about anything, you just call me," she said.

I knew that she meant that and I stood on the sidewalk and watched her walk into the lobby and give a box of cookies that she had ordered at the restaurant to the doorman. She waved to me as the elevator doors closed.

I walked the half-mile back to my apartment. I will never forget that walk, or the conversation that night. It had given me not only comfort about my situation but the impetus to "get on with it." It also showed me something about Eppie. This was the first time I had ever told her about a personal problem, asked for her advice, and how she handled it made me realize in a way I never had before why so many people for so many years had been turning to her column when their lives hit rough spots. She did not just provide a shoulder to cry on but also straight-from-the-hip directions to a smoother road.

That would not be the last conversation Eppie and I would have about divorce, hers or mine. I would later learn about what seemed to me Eppie's overwhelming generosity toward Jules after the divorce: having the cupboards of his and Elizabeth's Chicago apartment filled with food when they returned from their honeymoon; lending him money and investing in his later business ventures; helping financially with the daughter Jules and Elizabeth would have; paying for his care after he was hospitalized with a stroke and for the nursing-home care that followed. Seeing my amazed reaction at this apparently selfless largesse, she explained it simply: "Jules had been very good to me."

On January 21, 1999, at age eighty-one, Jules Lederer died

in his home in London. His obituaries boiled his life down to two accomplishments: "[He] founded one of the country's largest rental car companies and once was married to one of the world's best-known newspaper columnists." He requested that there be no services.

The playful twins (Eppie, left) as they appeared as seniors in the 1936 Central High School yearbook in Sioux City, Iowa.
(Courtesy of Sioux City Public Museum)

In matching gowns, Eppie (right) and Popo were married two days before their twenty-first birthdays in a lavish double ceremony in Sioux City in 1939. (Photo by Genelli Studios)

For her entire career Eppie
banged out her column
on an electric typewriter,
as she is seen doing here in her
apartment during the 1960s.
(*Chicago Sun-Times* file photo)

No one played a greater role in
Eppie's career than newspaper
editor Larry Fanning, who helped
mold her talent. She always
called him "good fortune smiling
on me." (*Chicago Sun-Times* file photo)

During a trip to Russia in 1959 Eppie played the role of foreign correspondent interviewing scores of people, such as this mother and daughter. (*Chicago Sun-Times* file photo)

As chair of the Easter Seals, Eppie met with President John Fitzgerald Kennedy in 1961. She later said of him, "Sex appeal oozed from every pore." (AP/Wide World Photos)

Eppie with some of the hundreds of owls, symbols of wisdom, that were given to her over the decades by friends, admirers, and others.
(*Chicago Sun-Times* file photo)

The face that launched a thousand columns. Even before becoming Ann Landers, Eppie was beguiling such famous folks as Walter Cronkite.
(*Chicago Sun-Times* file photo)

Eppie always felt a special connection and obligation to teenagers, such as this group gathered around her after a speech in suburban Chicago in 1962.
(*Chicago Sun-Times* file photo)

Eppie thought the war in Vietnam was "an immoral and impossible war" but was convinced by friend Hubert Humphrey to visit in 1967. (*Chicago Sun-Times* file photo)

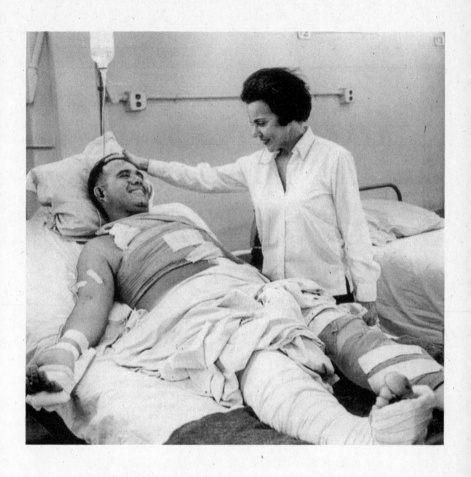

When she returned from Vietnam, where she visited
2,500 wounded soldiers, Eppie made hundreds
of comforting phone calls to the soldiers' relatives.
(*Chicago Sun-Times* file photo)

After an eight-year estrangement, Eppie and Popo (with husbands
Jules Lederer, right, and Mort Phillips, left) celebrated their
twenty-fifth wedding anniversaries in Bermuda.
(*Chicago Sun-Times* file photo)

Proud of her figure, Eppie was a demon for exercise,
whether walking up and down the stairs of her building
or, here, doing some stretching in the 1970s.
(*Chicago Sun-Times* file photo by Fred Stein)

When Eppie asked her female readers in a 1984 column whether they would prefer being held tenderly to making love, she received more than ninety thousand responses.

(*Chicago Sun-Times* file photo by Gene Pesek)

The biggest stars on the Chicago newspaper scene, Eppie and columnist Mike Royko, were seen here at a 1978 party. They were vastly different but shared a deep mutual respect. (Photo by Andrew Epstein)

Together again: the feuding and fussing long behind them, Eppie and Popo entertained some friends and had some laughs at Eppie's apartment in 1987. (*Chicago Tribune* photo by John Bartley)

Eppie was very fond of Bill and Hillary Clinton and often visited with them at the White House during his presidency. (White House Photos)

Jeanne Phillips (left) joined her mom in writing the "Dear Abby" column in 1987 and joined Popo here when she got a star on the Hollywood Walk of Fame in 2001. (AP/Wide World Photos)

Eppie's only child, Margo, started her journalism career by going "undercover" as a Playboy bunny. She now writes the syndicated "Dear Prudence" column. (top: *Chicago Tribune* file photo; bottom: *Chicago Tribune* photo by Allen Penn)

One of the last photos taken of Eppie standing in the living room of her apartment posing for a *Tribune Magazine* cover story in 2001. (*Chicago Tribune* photo by Chris Walker)

Dr. Nancy Wexler

HIGGINS PROFESSOR
OF NEUROPSYCHOLOGY—COLUMBIA
UNIVERSITY MEDICAL SCHOOL

New York City

My father was the first to meet Eppie. That was in 1978. He was a practicing psychologist who, a decade before, had started the Hereditary Disease Foundation, a nonprofit, basic science organization dedicated to the cure of genetic disease. He explained to Eppie that 100 percent of public contributions to the foundation went directly to support the scientific research. She was amazed and told him, "Wow. I'd like to be involved." She became a trustee of the foundation and remained one until her death.

She was an extraordinary woman. It's hard to use past tense with her because she was right there, a real presence, completely authentic, no airs, no manipulation. When she was with you she was totally focused on you, and I remember that from my first meeting with her. My mother had died a couple of years before I met her and she was wonderful about being sympathetic and comforting. She was warm, down-to-earth, and full of questions. She gave people advice for her entire life, but she wasn't somebody with just answers. She had a lot of questions, too, and she was willing to talk about her own feelings and about her own life. I really adored her.

She was also just terrific to be with. She had a fantastic capacity to have fun and really brought out the best in people. We had pajama parties at her apartment, and we'd both climb into bed with our pajamas on, eat chocolates, and talk about boyfriends, and all sorts of things. Yes, we eventually went to sleep, though she was a reverse day and nighter. She'd stay up late and get up late, and though I had the same kind of clock, she was very disciplined about getting up and doing exercises. She worked out every day, and she had the best figure.

Of course she was extremely intelligent, too. She took the right measure of people. She recognized that there were people who would use her, but she had a strong sense of herself. Once she was convinced you were a good person, she never doubted you. Eppie was like a flame for a moth, in a good way, an appealing way. Everybody wanted to be in her circle, to feel her warmth and vitality. Eppie just touched people. She was not afraid to get close.

She was completely wonderful about what she did for the foundation. A woman wrote to her and said, "I don't have animals. I'm not getting along with my kids, I want to leave money to a good charity, but there are so many that aren't good. Can you recommend a good charity?" Eppie wrote back and recommended our foundation, the Hereditary Disease Foundation, as well as the Salvation Army. She never told us. It just showed up in her column. We were stunned and overjoyed. All of a sudden people started calling us and naming us beneficiaries in their wills.

After that we got a call from a lawyer in Flint, Michigan. This gentleman had passed away. He was somewhat eccentric and had said in his will, "I want to give my money to that California Heredity Foundation." Our name wasn't in the will at all, but the deceased man's lawyer thought the man had intended the money for us. The man's children contested the will, arguing that the father did not know what he was doing. So they hired lawyers and we hired lawyers. Eventually, the lawyers discovered a safe deposit box and in it was Eppie's column about us. The judge ruled in our favor and the foundation received half a million dollars.

We still have gifts that come to us because of her column. Even now when people ask what the foundation is about we say, 'This is what Ann Landers had to say about us.' It's better than the Good Housekeeping Seal of Approval.

Eppie was magic. People trusted her and it really meant an enormous amount to her; to change people's lives for the better. She could have easily just sat back and put her feet up and smelled the roses instead of the coffee. But that wasn't her. She was always bustling around. It would have been wonderful to have a fraction of her ability to change the world for the better. Me? I'd take a pinky's worth.

Ben T.

REAL ESTATE INVESTOR

Los Angeles

The date? Of course I remember. It was August 23, 1959. I was in a bar in downtown San Francisco. It was eight in the morning and I was having a Scotch.

I didn't want to be there. I didn't want to be having a drink. I had an appointment to meet with one of my clients at eight and I just decided to come in this bar instead. I had been out late the night before, with some other clients, and, as usual, I had gotten drunk. This was my life. I was a salesman for a paper company. I was twenty-seven years old. I was married with a two-year-old little boy. I loved my wife and son, but I was losing my grip on them and on my life.

It wasn't easy being a salesman in those days. Basically, you did most of your sales over cocktails and I was good at that. You ever see that movie, *The Days of Wine and Roses*? That was my life. I was the good-time guy. I had the cash to buy the drinks, the expense account. I had the stories to tell, the dirty jokes, and then I get the sale.

But the drinking was really getting out of control. Sometimes after the clients went home, I'd stay in the bars until I was almost too drunk to walk. One night I got beat up and robbed by a couple of guys. They took the watch my wife gave me when we got married.

I knew something was wrong—I couldn't stop whenever I drank—but I didn't know what to do about it. My wife knew I was in trouble, especially when I came home drunk and passed out on the couch. She suggested that I go see our priest. I was a Catholic—still am—but when I went to see my priest and I told him that my drinking was out of control and that I needed help, he just sat there listening to me. Then he pointed out a couple of Bible passages and told me to read them every day. "God will give you the strength," he said.

Well, God wasn't doing anything for me, and that's what I was doing in that bar at 8 A.M. in San Francisco. My hands were shaking. My hangover was bad, and I remember that the bartender said, "You sure you want this?" when he brought my drink. I did and drank it fast and asked for another one. He brought it over and he also brought a newspaper. "Read this," he said, and he pointed to an "Ann Landers" column. It wasn't that day's paper. Maybe it was just something he kept around under the bar, but in the column was a letter from a guy talking about how his drinking was ruining his life. He sounded just like me. At the bottom of the column Ann Landers told the man about AA [Alcoholics Anonymous]. I had never hear of AA. Sounds impossible now, but it wasn't all that well-known then. I went to the phone book, found a number, and called. I went to my first meeting that day and I've been sober ever since.

Sounds simple but I really believe that Ann Landers, with a little help from that bartender—I went to him later and thanked him—saved my life. Maybe I would have found AA on my own. Maybe I would be dead. I've gone to a meeting every week since then, even if I've been out of town or out of the country. It's easy to find a meeting now anywhere.

I eventually got in the real estate business and did very well. I'm still married and we have three grandchildren and one great-grandchild. My life is good and I try to give back. I've been an AA sponsor for more than forty people over the years.

I'd been sponsoring this young guy, twenty-four, really nice young man and he was doing well. On the morning of July 23, he called me, and he caught me right in the middle of reading about Ann Landers's death. I was crying and he asked me what was wrong and I told him that Ann Landers had died and he said, "So?" I told him to meet me for coffee and that's when I told him the same story I'm telling you. At the end of the story he said, "Wow . . . I wonder how many other people out there could tell that same story?"

Dale Ludwig

PRESENTATION SKILLS TRAINER

Chicago

G rowing up on a farm in north-central Illinois you can feel pretty isolated. When I talk about it today, my friends are amazed that there were long stretches of days in the summer when I had no contact with anyone outside my family.

I had five brothers and sisters and two parents, so it wasn't that there was no one around to talk to, but this was a working farm. And we, my siblings and I, were part of the workforce. We were Protestants, after all, and of German heritage. Every day in the summer from the time I could read, until I was 16 and able to drive, mail delivery was a big part of my day. This is from 1960 to 1969. The mailman delivered nothing with my name on it, just a lot of farm magazines. My father subscribed to an endless line of them.

But we also got the daily newspaper, the *Rockford Morning Star*. It was the paper I was interested in. I'd always known that I would never live a farming life, so the paper provided contact with the rest of world. News of Vietnam, crime in Chicago, assassinations, race riots, the 1968 Democratic Convention—they all came into the house, into my life—through the *Morning Star.* Yes, we had a TV and radio, but they didn't offer the same intimacy that reading the paper did.

Around adolescence I got hooked on "Ann Landers." I loved the stories of cheating husbands, desperate alcoholics, lecherous ministers. This was great stuff. These people were real and unlike any others I knew. And the best part was how Ann treated them. Even when she suggested that they ship themselves off to counseling or told them to "Mind Your Own Business," there was a level of respect in her responses that gave every one of them dignity. These people were worthy of her attention and what she was telling them is that they really could change their lives if they just pulled themselves up by their bootstraps and got going.

I thrived on those letters and Ann's responses. Part of my isolation at this time had a lot to do with the fact that I was not only a kid growing up on a farm that held little interest for him, but I was also a gay kid growing up on a farm that held little interest for him. When I'm asked today if I was closeted the whole time I was growing up, I don't know what to say. I think, where are you before you are closeted? Wherever that is, that's where I was: a state of ignorance that precedes denial. But, like every gay kid, there was a part of me that knew I was different. And reading Ann Landers let me know that was okay, that I was okay.

I don't remember the exact dates the letters were printed or what the details were, but I do remember that she acknowledged and accepted the lives of gay people. Her column gave them a voice. And better than that, she advocated tolerance and understanding. There was no "You better straighten yourself out, Bub," to the guy who was questioning his sexual orientation. There was no "Get your son to a professional counselor before it's too late" to the anxious parents of a gay child. What she displayed was respect for gay people, almost always supporting it with a reference to one of her minister, rabbi, psychologist, or social worker friends. It was simple stuff, really, but for me in the late '60s, these columns were so compassionate and empowering. Especially coming from a woman of my parents' generation, the words of Ann Landers were more important than anything I read.

Professor Joseph Boskin

EMERITUS PROFESSOR OF
HISTORY AND URBAN STUDIES—
BOSTON UNIVERSITY

Boston

I believe that through "Ann Landers" columns you can trace the social history of the United States over the last half of the twentieth century. The letters in the column tell you what concerned people, what made them anxious, what made them frightened, what turned them on, and what turned them off.

I read her every day for as long as I can remember. I started reading her just as a lark, not as a historian. The column always fascinated me, and when I began teaching social history I used many of the letters from her columns in my classes.

I might select one because of its use of storytelling, such as one about the embarrassing secretary. It tells of a man who wakes up on his birthday and feels rejected. He's aging. He thinks he'll go down and have breakfast with his wife and she'll wish him happy birthday and give him a present. But when he goes down she doesn't say anything. So then he thinks, well, when my kids come down, they'll say something. But they're hurrying off to school. He goes to the office, and his secretary remembers his birthday. She gives him a present and asks him out to lunch. They have a couple of martinis and she says, "Come back to my place." So he does. And she disappears. Five minutes go by and the door bursts open and there's the man's wife and kids and his secretary singing "Happy Birthday." And he's sitting there with nothing on but his socks.

I usually had about two hundred fifty students in my class. When I would read the letter it was so quiet. At the end, the class erupted in laughter. Then I had the students analyze the story. It would always be an interesting discussion. Some were critical of the man, others of his secretary for leading him on.

It's clear that people responded to the column, to Ann Landers. When there were social changes taking place, she recognized what was going on. There are many varieties of "mainstream America" and she was not just the voice of one, but clearly tapped into most of them. Her column was a barometer in many ways. Some people would ask themselves what they would do if they were in circumstances similar to those of the letter writers. Others recognized themselves in those letters. People who wrote to Ann Landers were puzzled. They were concerned. They were telling her things that they wouldn't tell their pastor or their rabbi or minister, or any other people they know. They wanted an authoritative voice. She was anonymous; they were never going to see her; and Ann wanted nothing from them.

Her column was an easy read, not at all like reading

a news story, yet every one contained a story. She never put anyone down, was never snide but she could be caustic. She recognized human foibles and always allowed her humanity to come across. I felt such a loss when she died. She played a big role in the social behavior of this country in creating a dialogue that addressed the issues and concerns of the time. I was, always will be, fascinated by her. She was a unique American story. Is she buried in Chicago? I wouldn't mind going to her grave to talk with her for a while.

Paula Naggi

ASSOCIATE FACULTY MEMBER—
MT. SAN JACINTO COLLEGE

South California

I read Ann's column religiously every day, and she made such sense and seemed so approachable that I connected with her. She was kind of a cross between my mom and my nana; two great ladies who were kind and gentle when it was warranted, but could also knock you out of your complacency or tell you a thing or two when you needed to hear it.

I learned so much from her! She complemented the lessons taught to me by my parents, relatives, teachers, and clergy. She was in a position to share profound and important thoughts, essays, letters, and poems. I am not sure how old I was when I began reading Ann Landers. A particular column, however, changed my life. I was about fifteen when I read it, and going through the usual teenaged angst. I can't say what might have happened if I hadn't read the poem that was in her column that day—but I do know beyond the shadow of a doubt that its effect on me was profound and continues to resound.

"On this day,
  mend a quarrel.
Seek out a forgotten friend.
Dismiss a suspicion
  and replace it with trust.
Write a letter to someone
  who misses you.
Encourage someone
  who has lost faith.
Keep a promise.
Forget an old grudge.
Examine your demands on others
  and vow to reduce them.
Fight for a principle.
Express your gratitude.
Overcome an old fear.
Take two minutes to appreciate
  the beauty of nature.
Tell someone you love him.
Tell him again.
  And again.
  And again."

I clipped the poem out and put it in my wallet, where I carried it for many years. It has helped me to deal with difficult situations and find resolutions to problems. But more, it has assisted me in developing into the kind of person I wanted to be; a process which has proven to be a never-ending work in progress that is both a challenge and a sacred trust.

At nineteen, I met the love of my life. We married and had two sons. As a young bride, I learned patience and understanding. As a mother, I learned that in the same way I had been given unconditional love by my parents, I, too, loved my children without reservation. Ann's advice to never go to bed mad became a challenge to me on many occasions. In those moments, I would remember the last lines of the poem. When my first husband died of lymphoma at the age of forty, he knew just how much he was loved. Losing him really brought that early lesson home all over again. Now I have a second husband who was a bachelor until he was forty-two. The adjustment hasn't been an easy one; we've definitely had our share of difficulties. But the one thing he must know more than anything else is that I love him. I've come to the conclusion that knowing you are loved is the single most important ingredient for building a positive self-image and having a good life. Nothing else compares, not money, not success. Love is what it's all about.

After many years, Ann reprinted the poem, and again, I cut it out and replaced the old one, by then yellowed and frayed. With the passage of years, that copy, too, became illegible, but by then it had become such a part of me. This little poem, augmenting my religious upbringing, the unconditional love of my parents, and the never-ending sage advice from a woman I never had the honor to meet, became a blueprint for my life.

William Bryan Sorens

PRISONER

Huntsville, Texas

M y life before I read "Ann Landers" was as screwed up and depressing and just plain wrong as any life could get. I am a convicted criminal in Texas, now in my nineteenth year of incarceration (I have twelve to twenty-four more months to serve). I was a business and media professional before my arrest and conviction, and I never read the column. In fact, I was among the many detractors of "Ann Landers," lumping the column with other columns as being some kind of loser-confession vehicle and social phenomenon for the kind of person who needed to "get a life." I was so wrong, and as if to prove it, my own life was corrupt in ways that even the most troubled "Ann Landers" reader could never have imagined.

My job in media took me into the highest and lowest echelons of Dallas society. I rubbed shoulders with oil barons, real estate moguls, and some of the most talented and "beautiful" people in Texas. Many creative folks I met lived on the fringe of society, engaging in all manner of extreme behavior, and I joined them. I cavorted with producers, directors, and local "stars," as well as with many "wanna-bes," from strippers to hanger-oners. I began sacrificing my marriage and family to be with them, and eventually I created my own, particular form of extremism. I even started photographing the Dallas underworld at night, and then began partaking of it.

Life essentially came to an end for me when I was arrested, and most tragically and even worse, my poor choices and way of life affected those good and innocent people in my life. Prison was, however, the final wake-up call that I had to make some changes, unless I wanted to continue to live literally a damned life without regard for others. I knew this way of life would eventually kill me, too.

In prison, I began reading everything I could get my hands on concerning life change and self-improvement. I wanted to know the hard truth about everything that went into my awful thinking and choices. I enrolled in the prison's visiting grad school program of the University of Houston-Clear Lake. My grad studies forced me to read even more. My newspaper habit became even more important. I discovered Eppie— "Ann Landers"—for the first time. At first I simply skimmed her columns, hesitant and even embarassed at myself to be looking at it. But Eppie slowly took hold as I realized that real people with real problems, not so unlike my own, were writing in and getting real answers from her.

"Ann Landers" became a much-anticipated part of my days. The column opened me up to being genuinely human— to being fully emotional, fully cognitive, and fully moral. By reading about the problems of others, I began to put my own in perspective. I began to lose my selfishness and self-centeredness and ego. I began to understand that compassion toward others was a foundation for my own healing and transformation. There is real freedom to be found by letting one's life be touched by others—by others' needs and hurts and troubles and, thank God, celebrations. Many times I'd stop reading and think, "No wonder she does this for a living." I found not only helpful instruction, general insights, and conventional as well as unconventional wisdom, but humor, joy, and a degree of fulfillment.

"Ann Landers" was no mere column in my life. Eppie became like a dear friend, as I am certain she was for thousands of others who never actually knew her. As my smart, brave, compassionate, creative, and funny friend, I cannot imagine my life without her influence, especially inside this hell called prison where there are no such friends. Maybe, above all, it was Eppie's irrepressible, contagious optimism that made her the beloved Ann Landers. No matter the problem, there was a solution. No matter the circumstances, there was a way to rise above them. Could there have been any better, more consoling, more hopeful message for one such as I?

Florence Boughner

GROUP LEADER—RECOVERY, INC.

Cleveland

My life was an awful mess. Period. I was always depressed, in and out of hospitals.

In the late summer of 1968, I was working for a commercial real estate agency in Cleveland. Some days I would just stay in bed rather than go to work. Maury Lewis was my boss, a wonderful and understanding man. He had a beautiful wife, Blanche, who suffered from terminal lung cancer and could scarcely pull herself through the door. But on those days when I couldn't get out of bed, Blanche would call me and say, "Florence, get out of that bed, clean up, and get your clothes on. We need you!"

Some days that would work. I could tell that Maury and Blanche were very worried about me, as were my family and friends. I was worried, too. I don't need to tell you how high the suicide rate is among chronically depressed people. I am positive that I was on my way to becoming part of those sad statistics. Then one morning at work Maury handed me an "Ann Landers" column. It contained a letter from a woman with anxiety who was unable to leave her home. Ann told her about a self-help group called Recovery, Inc., explaining that there was no fee and that the group offered help to people with all sorts of emotional and nervous problems. Ann was typically firm in her response. She never merely suggested but would write, "They are listed in the phone book. Find a meeting and go!" She steered many people that way, whether to AA, Overeaters Anonymous, or in my case Recovery, Inc. And she would often say to the letter writers, "Please let me know how things have worked out." That was so optimistic. It gave hope.

That's what I said to Maury after reading the column: "It's a hope." He replied, "Hope nothing—get there."

There was a meeting very close to our home and, of course, being in total denial about my problem, it took me a long time to totally "dig in." But the seed was planted by that wonderful, wise woman, Ann Landers. At first I was skeptical. I did not keep that column that I now believe saved my life, because at the time I thought nothing could ever help me. But once Recovery, Inc., took hold and I understood the recovery "method" as it is called, I knew it was a lifesaver. I continued with meetings. I became an assistant group leader eleven years ago and now have led my own meeting for five years.

I honestly believe that if I hadn't been touched by Ann's words, I wouldn't be here today. Literally. Compare me now to the old days and you would never suspect I ever had a problem. If I could send you a picture it would show a very content Florence, sitting on her piano bench with the flowers from her forty-fourth wedding anniversary and smiling serenely.

I sincerely regret that I never took time to sit down and formally thank Ann Landers, as I should have. I loved the column and seldom missed it. I think she was one of the wisest, most caring, helpful, sincere women. I felt I knew her personally, like I could sit across the breakfast table with her, coffee in hand, and tell her anything without embarrassment. She certainly was a remarkable woman, and I quietly thank her every day for the life I have.

Bob McBee

PUBLIC AFFAIRS EXECUTIVE, RETIRED

San Antonio

I had been transferred recently to Chicago and I was working for the Veterans Administration (VA), now the Department of Veterans Affairs. Every year during the week of Valentine's Day the VA had programs and events to salute hospitalized veterans. I went to work early one morning— maybe too early—and was thinking of ideas of what they could do differently. All of a sudden it came to me: "What if I got Ann Landers to have people send valentines to hospitalized vets?"

I had always read her column. She was effective. And she had a great record of doing things for veterans. She was always very supportive of them. My boss liked the idea so we wrote a letter to her and then I walked it over to her office at the *Tribune,* which was about eight blocks away. I met her assistants, Kathy Mitchell and Marcy Sugar, and asked them to make sure that Ann got the letter. An hour later they called. They had already talked to Ann and gotten the go-ahead, and discussed the best way to announce it.

It was a collaborative effort. What she wanted was for the VA to write a letter about "Valentines for Vets" and then she would enthusiastically endorse the idea and ask readers to follow through. She wanted the letter to come from me, but my boss thought such a letter should come from Washington, D.C., and so the Secretary of the VA signed the letter.

She told us what she liked and didn't like about the letter. We fixed it up and she ran it in her column. At the end of her response she wrote, "Send your valentine because I'm sending mine." I called her office immediately and said, "If she's really going to send a valentine, it'll get lost in the pile of mail." I said I'd take care of that. I was a former journalist, used to work for the *Kansas City Star*, and I knew a guy at Hallmark. He sent me some blank cards to use. I wrote a greeting from her and got her signature and printed up a bunch of them. We decided to send them to all the World War I veterans that first year. At one of the hospitals this World War I vet said, "I just got a valentine from Ann Landers. Why would she send me a valentine?" He seemed a little confused but so touched and happy.

So the next year we decided that every vet would get a valentine from Ann Landers. We'd make sure that every vet got one with his breakfast or dinner tray. It was set up so that all the valentines would be mailed to one central location, at Hines Hospital in the Chicago suburbs.

The column ran during the second weekend in January. Within a month, the cards were pouring into Hines. There were two million of them. Hines had to have volunteers come in to help sort them into boxes and ship them off to the different hospitals: 171 of them.

Eppie—she told me to call her Eppie the first time we ever talked—was vivacious, friendly, spunky, easy to talk to. I don't think she got enough credit for what she did with this program. It's a great program. But whenever we would be together and someone would ask how the program got started, she always pointed to me and said, "He did it all." I appreciated that.

During the Gulf War she called me and asked what could she do for the troops or send to them, and I called the Department of Defense and they gave me a list of the standard gifts people could send and she printed that list. And one year she called and said, "You know I have a lot of people who read my column in Canada. A lot of vets. Can we distribute the valentines to them, too?" I went to the Canadian consulate and they arranged for it.

I retired in 1994. "Valentines for Vets" had been going for five years. In that time we received more than ten million cards. I figure that each vet got three to five of them every year. And some people sent candy. The heir to the Tootsie Roll fortune, who I think was a friend of Eppie's, sent Tootsie Rolls. The Chocolate House in Milwaukee sent pounds of chocolates.

Many years later when I was in the hospital for thyroid surgery Eppie tried to call. But the people at the hospital didn't believe she was who she said she was: "Ann Landers." She finally got one of her assistants to make the call and she got through and gave me hell, in a joking way, for "refusing" to take her call. She just wanted to see how I was doing.

She was just that kind of person. I remember, the second year of the "Valentines for Vets" program, that I got a call from Eppie and she said, "Bob, I want to go to the hospitals and visit and hand out the valentines."

There was a huge snowstorm, but when I pulled up in front of the Hines Hospital she was waiting there, sitting in the back of her limo. She and I went to the spinal cord injury ward. Oh, that's a hard place to visit. But she spent a lot of time talking to each of the vets. Then she went up and visited people in the other wards.

She was so caring and so much fun. Every year after that, the hospital staff would set up which vets she'd visit. She'd visit almost all the wards and stay for a long time. I remember at one of the hospitals they used to have music therapy classes and when she came through the door the vets serenaded her with this one tune. They sang, "I Just Called to Say I Love You." And all of a sudden she started to dance, just twirling around the floor all by herself in front of all these smiling veterans. I guess she just loved to dance.

12

· LOT 1248W ·

A Collection of Awards Presented to
Eppie Lederer

On the wall of famed columnist Mike Royko's office in the Tribune Tower was a quote from Samuel Johnson: "No man but a blockhead ever wrote except for money."

Mike had moved to the *Tribune* in 1984—when Australian media mogul Rupert Murdoch purchased the *Sun-Times*. He was the most prominent among sixty-eight people to resign in the wake of the purchase. Some went directly to the *Tribune,* which was eager to have them; some went to work for other papers; some retired; some changed careers. Mike was the biggest catch for the *Tribune*. His five-day-a-week column was a city fixture. Whether he was taking on crooked politicians, mobsters, exasperating bureaucracy, cultural oddities, or the strange twists of contemporary life, his column was honest and direct and reflected the city in all its two-fisted charm. It was tremendously popular here and in the hundreds of papers in which it was syndicated.

One afternoon in 1987 I was sitting with Mike in his fourth-floor office. We had just played handball at a club nearby, and now we were talking about Eppie, because the day before Mike had been told by a high-ranking editor some news that would not be made public for another two weeks: Eppie was coming to the *Tribune*.

"I like Eppie. She's a good broad," Mike said.

I had left the *Sun-Times* when Royko did and spent a few years writing a couple of books and trying to write a couple of others. But the pull of newspapers was great, and for the previous six months I had been writing freelance stories and reviews for the *Tribune*, which would hire me as TV critic in 1988. Mike and I had become good friends when were both working for the *Daily News* and, after that paper folded in 1978, when we both moved to the *Sun-Times*. I saw him at least once a week, for drinks or handball, or tennis, or golf, or dinners. Eppie I saw less often. She didn't come in much to the *Sun-Times* offices when I worked there, preferring to work at home or on the road during her frequent out-of-town trips. When we did bump into each other, it was always a pleasant experience, since she almost always gave me a compliment about a recent story I had written, and I told her she looked great.

That day Mike and I first discussed Eppie's coming to the *Tribune,* we started to count the number of people who had left the *Sun-Times* in the previous few years but we stopped after a few minutes. The list was getting too long. "Eppie's leaving will hurt," Mike said. "She'll bring a lot of readers over here. I'm glad she's coming. Now, all those wackos who've been writing to me with their problems can write to her."

On the surface, Mike and Eppie appeared to be as different as two people could possibly be. Mike's office in the Tribune Tower contained ashtrays piled with cigarette butts, the odd golf club or two, maybe a tennis racket, books and newspapers stacked randomly in piles, and a life-sized cutout of John Wayne as he had appeared in *The Searchers*. Wayne was one of Mike's heroes. "His movies make me feel good," he wrote. "John Wayne shot people in the heart, and drank whiskey, and treated his horse like a horse. He treated women like he treated his horse. He seemed real because he reminded me of the men in my neighborhood. . . . We knew he would not become bogged down in red tape, or fret about losing his pension rights, or cringe when his boss looked at him." Sometimes Mike would put this John Wayne cutout in the shower that was in his private bathroom and would delight when a scream erupted from some unsuspecting bathroom user behind the closed door.

Eppie's office at the *Sun-Times* had been painted a bright pink. The *Tribune* digs would be less garish. She would have a large office to herself, with dark wood paneling, a soft couch, a couple of leather chairs, a glass-topped desk and coffee table. Though there were many books on the shelves behind the desk and a few framed photos scattered about, as well as some owl figurines, the office was not a place of clutter. She, too, had a private bathroom and shower. But if Mike's office had the rumpled look and feel of that of a gas-station manager, Eppie's might have been the office of a small-town bank president.

As different as they were, Mike and Eppie shared many important characteristics, some due to fate and some fundamental. Both had been discovered and given columns by Larry Fanning, and though the columns were not at all alike, both writers worked at them ferociously, Mike writing five days a week and Eppie seven. Mike and Eppie were both of an "old school," more closely tied to the *Front Page* days of Chicago newspapers than to what the business was becoming in the 1980s and 1990s.

"This business used to be fun, and so were the people in it," Eppie told me more than once over dinner, echoing Mike's words in a 1996 radio interview when he said, "There is a great deal about the newspaper business I miss. A great deal of the fun and the spirit have gone out of working for a newspaper. The major change is the kind of people who work on newspapers. . . . There was more of a sense that a newspaper was family. If someone got a story on page one, you'd say, 'Good story,' and not, 'Why not me?' You never heard the word *career* in the old days."

They didn't see each other often as their social circles rarely intersected, but they shared a deep mutual respect. She asked him to join dozens of world-renowned experts as a contributor to *The Ann Landers Encyclopedia A to Z.* His contribution was a reprinted column, "How to Cure a Hangover," which began, "A hangover is nature's way of telling you that you got drunk. I've never understood why nature goes to the bother, since millions of wives pass on the information."

Mike drank. Eppie didn't. Mike, who had won a Pulitzer Prize in 1971, hated flying. Eppie loved it. He eschewed the honorary degrees and lesser awards routinely offered to him. Eppie eagerly accepted them and had a pile. Mike was syndicated in some six hundred papers. Eppie was in twelve hundred. He was a Chicago icon. She was an international one.

By the time Eppie moved to the *Tribune,* she was able to command $10,000 lecture fees, though she cut back considerably on her appearance schedule during the 1980s, perhaps because her social calendar was jam-packed and would remain so until she got sick and died. She frequently attended charitable dinners in cities across the country and was on the guest list for White House dinners and millionaires' birthday parties. She was also a favorite houseguest of such friends as columnist Art Buchwald and his wife, Ann, and Walter and Betsy Cronkite on Martha's Vineyard, where she loved to kick back. "I used to go to Paris or Rome or London. Now I can go anywhere I want to, but I have no interest in [traveling the world. I go] someplace quiet where I can go barefoot, and I don't have to dress up or get my hair fixed," she said about her life in the mid-1980s.

Five years after her divorce, her romantic life was an active one. "You bet I have gentlemen friends," she told a magazine writer in 1980. "But I'm not a swinger. I've never been interested in trying this, trying that. I date no one in Chicago. Here I'm all business. I have a few escorts but there's no romance. My dating is in other big cities. I have four or five very interesting friends." She said that she judged the men in her life by the chocolate they brought her. As for sex, she said, "In my pamphlet *Teen-age Sex and 10 Ways to Cool It,* I advise 'four feet on the floor and all hands on deck.' That applies to [me] as well. I'm a pretty square old lady." She doubted that she would ever marry again but said she wanted to spend time with men who were in "good physical condition, bright, stimulating, honest, preferably a non-smoker, someone who cerebrates at a very high level and whose own success wouldn't be overwhelmed by mine."

One of the few people seemingly not overwhelmed by Eppie's success was her sister Popo. Though they remained professional rivals, their personal relationship appeared to be have been close and affectionate for nearly two decades following their highly publicized first feud. In 1978 Eppie published *The Ann Landers Encyclopedia A to Z,* her most ambitious and interesting book, a 1,212-page gathering of essays from experts and other people notable in their fields, offering information on hundreds of subjects, from Abortion to Zoonoses—Diseases Humans Get from Animals. The book made its way to all the best-seller lists.

If rumors still circulated that Eppie and Popo were nonspeaking, bitter rivals, Eppie's acknowledgment in the *Ann Landers Encyclopedia* should have put them to rest: "A low bow to my twin, Popo Phillips ('Dear Abby'), for putting her book in cold storage so that I might have a clear field for mine. How's that for sisterly love?"

But they still made great copy for the press. In 1980, the *Ladies Home Journal* ran a profile of Eppie written by Cliff Jahr. It covered familiar territory, what had become by this time a kind of standard Eppie story: her thoughts about the advice business; the changing moral landscape of the country; her divorce, and her social life afterward. Naturally, Jahr asked Eppie to talk about the first feud with her sister and Eppie responded as she usually did, saying that, yes, she had been disappointed when Popo had started her column but that she no longer resented it and that she and her sister were as close as ever. It was an innocuous story.

That would not be true of the story that Jahr wrote for the magazine eighteen months later. His interview/profile of Popo was, for reasons that have never been clearly explained (Eppie was reluctant to ever talk about it with me), shocking. The story was peppered with barbs from Popo about Eppie's plastic surgery ("If she looked old, if she needed a face-lift, believe me it's because she needed it . . . when you cry a lot, it's got to show"); Jules ("He got tired of being Mr. Landers"); Eppie's chances of remarrying ("She's looking for a man with Jules' spark, and she ain't going to find him"); and other personal matters. Oddly, the same story had Popo saying, "[Eppie] is my best friend and I am hers."

Once the magazine hit newsstands, Popo publicly claimed she had been misquoted, prompting Jahr to say he had the entire interview on tape. Eppie, to her credit, said nothing in response, at least not publicly. But her readers did not stay silent. Her office was deluged in mail, suggesting that Popo had been drinking or even drunk during the interview; that she seek immediate professional help; and that she was jealous of Eppie. Whatever the reasons for Popo's comments, Eppie would not allow them to destroy the relationship and despite the traumas they had caused each other and the intensity of their professional rivalry, they still remained, in a very real sense, the playful, precocious girls from Sioux City.

That's what they appeared to be when they went back together to Sioux City in 1986 for their fiftieth high school class reunion. Checking into the Hilton, they were greeted by reporters and photographers. "We've been anonymous and we've been famous," Popo said. "And it's more fun famous." *Washington Post* reporter Elizabeth Kastor had been sent to cover the event and she interviewed a woman, LaVerne Hoof, who had taught the twins in Spanish class. "There was a splash wherever they went," Hoof said. "And they were very, very good, exceptional students." One of their classmates begged to differ, telling Kastor, "They talked all the time. Teachers always had to hush them." And another class-mate tried to put things in perspective, saying, "They're just two graduates, and there's a lot of us. There are a lot of other people in our class who have done something." Those who had done some-thing and those who had done comparatively little sat at the reunion dinner and listened to Eppie's speech: "If you have a good name, if you are right more often than you are wrong, if your chil-dren respect you, if your grandchildren are glad to see you, if your friends can count on you and you can count on them in times of trouble, if you can face your God and say 'I have done my best,' then you are a success."

Well into her third decade on the advice beat she tried to do her best in the column. Eppie certainly realized that help for many of the problems that had been featured in her column was becoming more easily accessible for most Americans. Though it might have been tempting to turn on professional cruise control, it was important to Eppie that she remain relevant for millions of people. Reading her had become a daily habit and one hard to break. Though many more advice columns were available—among them, Judith Martin's "Miss Manners" and Dr. Joyce Brothers—"Ann Landers" and "Dear Abby" still dominated the field, and Eppie was determined to keep it that way.

She was willing to take up new challenges and causes, aware that she was able to mold public opinion. In 1982, in response to a letter writer asking her to take a stand on nuclear disarmament, she urged her readers to write to President Reagan and express their opinions.

The response—more than a hundred thousand letters—was so great that it prompted a personal note from the president to Eppie. Reagan wrote: "Ann, we have tried many times since World War II to persuade the Russians to join us in reducing or even eliminating nuclear weapons, with little success. Perhaps instead of sending your copies to me, your readers should send copies of your column to Soviet President Leonid Brezhnev." That's what she suggested in a subsequent column, and she put her clout and connections to good use by having another of her influential friends, industrialist Armand Hammer, personally put a copy of the column in Brezhnev's hands.

She retained her uncanny ability to tap into the American psyche, especially when it came to matters of sex. On November 4, 1984, she asked her readers if they preferred being held tenderly to making love. It did not seem a particularly incendiary question but more than ninety thousand women responded. When all the responses were tallied, the results were that 72 percent of the women preferred cuddling to having sex. Eppie was not surprised by those figures but was flabbergasted by the number of responses.

The survey's method did have its detractors. Dr. Ruth

Westheimer, host of a radio program called "Sexually Speaking," said, "A survey like this is dangerous because of its implications. You don't know whether people want to be hugged for a month, for a while or forever. What [the survey] indicates is how many people read Ann Landers, and that's great."

They read her—and responded to the tune of 67,588 replies—when she later put the same question to her male readers. Of those, only about 8 percent, almost all of them older than sixty, said they would prefer cuddling to making love.

Mike Royko read Eppie's column in the *Sun-Times,* and before she reached out to her male readers he decided to conduct a survey of his own in print, one that Eppie would later tell me was one of the funniest things she had ever read. He started his *Tribune* column:

> "I hope nobody blushes, but I am going to pose a rather personal question to male readers. Given a choice, men, would you rather be having sex with your wife or out bowling with your buddies?
>
> "If you aren't a bowler, just substitute fishing, golf, shooting pool, leaning on a bar, watching TV or whatever your favorite recreational activity is.
>
> "This question was inspired by something my friend Ann Landers recently wrote. . . . The only complaint that I have about [the survey] is that it was directed only at females.
>
> "But, then, aren't most sex surveys?
>
> "Nobody ever asks us about our needs, our frustrations, our longings and yearnings. It's always: 'Madam, do you have your quota of orgasms? Does your husband

engage in an adequate amount of foreplay? Does the Earth shake?'

"We have become the forgotten sex, except during the recently endured Age of the Wimp, when many modern men didn't wait to be asked but blubbered out their most embarrassing thoughts to anybody who would tolerate them.

"But the average guy is never asked about such things. So, to provide some balance to Ann's survey, I am conducting my own."

In less than a week, Royko's mailbox was filled with nearly ten thousand letters. He wrote, "The response to my Sex or Bowling survey of men has been so huge that it will be days before we can scientifically tabulate the results and read the thousands of shocking letters."

Royko devoted the next few days to those responses, such as these: "When it comes to sex with my wife or bowling, I prefer sex with my wife because I don't have to change my shoes"; "If all my wife wants is cuddling and petting, she don't need me. She can go to the pet shop"; "I have a neighbor who prefers bowling to sex with his wife. So when he goes bowling, I have sex with his wife"; and, from a fellow calling himself Old 88 in Cleveland, "When I was young and in my prime/I'd rather swing my golf club anytime/But now that I am old and gray/I'd rather have sex twice a day. P.S. If you print this and get deluged with fan mail, please refer my phone number to females age 70 and over."

Finally Royko wrote, "The results of my Sex or Bowling survey are in, and the figures have been tabulated . . . and it came out this way: Sex: 66 percent. Bowling, drinking, golfing, cuddling or just about anything else: 22 percent. Others (which includes those who couldn't make up their minds or took this as an opportunity to write a creepy note to my secretary): 12 percent. Nor does the figure include several hundred angry female persons who wrote to condemn me as a male chauvinist pig. (I will deal sternly with them in a future column.)"

Eppie's move to the *Tribune* was a big deal. She was able to leave the *Sun-Times* because Murdoch, after little more than two years of ownership, sold the newspaper, as well as its News America Syndicate. That freed Eppie from her contract with the syndicate and allowed her to negotiate as a free agent. She worked out a deal with the Los Angeles Times Syndicate and Creators Syndicate. The deal finally gave her the rights to the name Ann Landers.

At the time, *Tribune* editor Jim Squires said in a statement, "The *Tribune* is delighted to welcome Ann Landers to the finest lineup of journalism talent anywhere. This is where she belongs. She is icing on the cake. . . . The fact that Eppie is a longtime Chicagoan who built a magnificent career here has naturally made her the best-read columnist in Chicago and the grande dame of Chicago journalism. In addition to her grace and prestige, we expect her to bring a lot of readers."

In that same statement, Eppie said, "After a great deal of consideration, I have decided to move my column to the *Chicago Tribune.* This was not an easy decision, since the *Sun-Times* has been my happy home for thirty-one years. The sale of the syndicate provided me with an opportunity to make another change in my life. I look forward to serving my readers with the same dedication and enthusiasm that has been my trademark since 1955."

The *Tribune* was one of about thirty papers across the United States that would be running both "Ann Landers" and "Dear Abby," which had been in the *Tribune* since 1973, after Popo's longtime home paper, *Chicago Today,* folded. That didn't faze Squires, who said, "There is a great reader demand for personal advice. And each columnist has developed her own distinct style and her own large and loyal following." Eppie took what had been "Dear Abby"'s spot, prominent placement on page two of the paper's daily feature section, "Tempo," as Popo's column moved back in the section, where it sits to this day, alongside the comics. This might have angered Popo, but there was no amount of lobbying she could have done to alter the situation, and so there was no outcry or argument from her West Coast offices.

The *Sun-Times,* in what many considered a master stroke of public relations, launched a contest to fill Eppie's job. "WANTED: GUIDANCE, GUTS & GOOD ADVICE" trumpeted full-page ads in the *Sun-Times* and *USA Today.* In short order, the paper heard from more than twelve thousand applicants. They were as young as four and as old as eighty-five. They sent in photos, résumés, sample columns, and letters.

Among the twelve thousand were convicts, an actress, lawyers, and a commodities trader. Their number was trimmed to 108, all of whom were given four sample letters—about obesity, AIDS, chutzpah, and a man who suspected his wife of having a yen for his brother—written by editors. On April 1, the field was narrowed to twenty-two.

A panel was formed—four mental health professionals, a news analyst, and a clergyman—and charged with picking six finalists. Their columns were to run in the paper, and, after readers registered their preference, the paper's editors would select the new columnist.

Jeffrey Zaslow was one of five men to make the finals. He said, "I'm 28 but have the wisdom of a 29-year-old." He was a staff correspondent for the *Wall Street Journal*. Raised in Philadelphia, Zaslow said he'd been a "contrary wise guy" ever since his mother, who wrote and directed a soap opera for cable TV, entered him at eighteen months as "Hercules Untrained" in the Atlantic City Baby Parade contest, which he won. In place of Eppie's famous experts, he said he would impanel an "average Joe advisory board made up of Joe the steelworker, Joe the bill collector, Josephine the telephone operator"—all real and all personal friends.

The search took four months. In June, the winner was named. Actually there were two winners: Zaslow and forty-seven-year-old Diane Crowley, a divorced lawyer, former teacher, mother of two and, not incidentally, the daughter of the original Ann Landers, Ruth Crowley.

Zaslow's column would be called "All That Zazz." It would be, its author said, "off the wall. . . . Some days I might just give unsolicited advice to the famous." Crowley's column would be "Your Problems," and its author said, "I've done divorces, I've done adoptions . . . [I have] a lot of experience in solving problems for people." Their columns debuted on July 1, 1987.

When the rival columns first appeared, Eppie told a reporter, "These people have no idea what's involved. It's an enormously demanding job. You not only have to know who the authorities are, you have to be able to get to them. . . . If they think it's going to be overnight fame and fortune, forget it."

· LOT 2693 ·

F.V.C., American Twentieth Century
A Portrait of Ann Landers, 1993

In the last decade of the twentieth century, if a person was given the dubious distinction of being named editor of the "Tempo" section of the *Tribune,* that person became, technically, Eppie's boss. There were many less-pleasant and more-demanding duties involved with running the paper's daily feature section: generating ideas that you hoped might turn into readable stories; listening to writers talk about their lousy marriages and problems with alcohol, and offering a myriad of other excuses why they would not be filing their stories on time; sitting in meetings, meetings, and more meetings; filling out personnel evaluations; answering calls from readers upset that the Brenda Starr comic strip "doesn't seem as good as it was forty-five years ago" or who wanted to argue about the correct meaning of "umbra," which was the answer to twenty-three across in the previous Thursday's crossword puzzle.

Having only a hint of these and other potential irritations, when I became "Tempo" editor in September 1994, the first person I called was Eppie. It was a courtesy call, to be sure, but a reassuring call as well. I was familiar with Eppie's reputation as a prolific and popular writer who would need little coddling or special attention, and cause no sleepless nights. "I've heard the news," Eppie said when I called. "And I'm delighted and wouldn't your father think this was interesting? I know he'd be pleased. So I want you to tell me exactly what you think of the column. Be honest. And come over for tea as soon as you can."

A few weeks later, on a breezy afternoon, I walked over to Eppie's building. I was a bit nervous because I had not, and did not want to admit that I had not, been a regular reader of Eppie's column. I was aware that each day's column arrived via computer in the features department about five weeks before it was scheduled to run—sent there, and to 1,199 other papers by Creators Syndicate in California. A few days before each column was scheduled to run, an editor on the copy desk would read it, punch some keys to set it in the correct format, slap a headline on it, and ship it out, again via computer, to the *Tribune*'s printing plant. "It comes in clean as a whistle," I was told by those on the copy desk, meaning it needed little if any editing.

As had been Eppie's way since the days of Larry Fanning,

she liked to have an editor on staff read the column before it was sent to Creators. Since she arrived at the *Tribune* in 1987, her editor had been Dennis Gosselin, a veteran newspaperman and editor of the *Tribune's Sunday Magazine*. "Let's just use that word *editor* in quotes," he told me, before my meeting with Eppie. "I just look things over, maybe make a comment now and then. Eppie's column won't be a worry for you. You'll have plenty of other things to give you headaches."

Eppie was holding the apartment door open when I got off the elevator on the fifteenth floor. She was dressed in a pretty, form-fitting blue dress that looked better suited to a dinner party than what was, essentially, an afternoon business meeting. I was glad I had worn a coat and tie. I extended my hand, but she ignored it and moved close to give me a kiss on the cheek. She said, "I'm so glad you're here. Come into the living room."

The room was larger than I remembered. But that was understandable, since this was only my second visit to the apartment. Three years earlier I had attended Margo's fiftieth birthday party there and spent most of the time sitting in a room at the back of the apartment catching up with friends.

Tea went well, a thirty-minute conversation that mostly consisted of catching up, personally and professionally. I was impressed and flattered that she knew so much about my career. It had been more than a decade since we worked together at the *Sun-Times*. She had obviously done some research. How else would she have been able to bring up the first story I ever wrote for the *Sun-Times*, a review of a book called *How to Get a Teenage Boy and What to Do with Him When You Get Him*? I was sixteen when I wrote that.

"I remember that," Eppie said. "It was a good review."

I was speechless. Maybe I even blushed.

"Now, tell me how your mother is," she said. "Does she miss your father terribly?"

And on it went, until she said, "Well, do you think you should get back? You're an editor now, and I'm sure you've got a lot of things to deal with more important than me."

I could take what I thought was a hint and started to get up off the couch.

"But don't you have time for a quick tour?" she asked. "I know you didn't get to see the whole place at Margo's party."

Eppie's apartment was filled with art and fine furniture, dozens of owl figurines, hundreds of photos, expensive vases, paintings, keys to cities, and the most astonishing collection of personal photographs I ever expect to see. They covered a large portion of the hallway's eastern wall. "This is what I call the 'wall of fame,'" Eppie said casually. Most of the photos were in plain eight-by-ten frames, the sort one might buy at any department store or at Wal-Mart: Eppie with Jimmy Carter, with Ronald Reagan, Bill and Hillary Clinton, Robert Redford, Richard Nixon, Helen Hayes, Kirk Douglas, Mike Wallace, Henry Fonda, Muhammad Ali, and dozens of others. It appeared to me that the photos had been arranged randomly, without any chronological, professional, or aesthetic order. I was immediately drawn to two photos hung side by side in the middle of the wall: Eppie getting hugged by Nelson Mandela next to a picture of her getting kissed while being lifted off the ground by Michael Jordan. How many celebrities, even today, could boast such a varied collection?

During the quick tour, I also saw paintings by Chagall, Picasso, and Renoir; wall panels and sconces imported from England; intricately sculpted ceilings; French and English antiques and reproductions; candelabra and chandeliers; a lovely oil portrait of Eppie; Chinese vases carved with flowers and birds; a Steinway piano made of walnut; and all sorts of other eye-catching items. It was a bit overwhelming until we got to her office. It was a mess. I felt right at home amid the clutter of books, magazines, and newspapers. Her desk, on which sat an electric typewriter, was piled with mail.

"I still use the typewriter," Eppie said. "I know it would be easier if I got into the computer age. Just call me old-fashioned."

"Old-fashioned is good," I said.

We walked into the bathroom. It was huge, with mirrors on the walls. It was dominated by a large marble bathtub. "I had shelves specially built into that tub," she said. "That's where I do a lot of work. I pile letters on the shelves and read them while I'm soaking. I can stay in this tub for two hours." She said she could read as many as eight hundred letters in that time. "I don't read each in its entirety. After all this time, I know what's going on from the first few sentences. They are so stimulating that I have to make myself go to bed."

"What time do you go to bed?" I asked.

"I'm really a night owl. That's something you should know," Eppie said. "So if you need me, don't call before noon."

I called her every few weeks, usually around three in the afternoon. I would say, "How are you, dear?" She would say, "Fine. Do you think the column's on target?" I would say, "Yes, oh yes." And that was about that, until about six months later when she called me and asked, "Do you think that someone at 'Tempo' might write about my new book? The publisher said they called and someone told them you wouldn't be doing anything on the book. That just didn't sound right to me, so I thought I'd ask. If you don't want to, that's okay."

"We want to. We want to," I said. "I don't know who would have said no."

The book was titled *Wake Up and Smell the Coffee! Advice, Wisdom and Uncommon Good Sense.* It was her first book in ten years, more than justifying a story.

Surprisingly, when I was debating which of the "Tempo" staff writers might be best suited to write this story, one of the senior editors called me into his office and said, "If you're really serious about doing a story about this book, we can't afford to make it seem like a puff piece. It's got to be tough on her. We don't want to look like we're promoting one of our own. So you write the story. You're the 'Tempo' editor. You understand the politics. And make sure you ask her if she thinks she's still relevant."

"Relevant? Why don't I just call all of the twelve hundred editors of the papers that run her column, including this one, and ask them if they think she's still relevant?" I said.

"Very funny," he said. "Just don't make it too nice."

When I got to Eppie's apartment to interview her about the new book and her career, a crew from *The Oprah Winfrey Show* was there, videotaping furniture and photos for a later broadcast that would feature Eppie.

"Jay Leno called," Eppie said.

Well of course Jay Leno called. Being Ann Landers meant—

among many, many things—that when celebrities like Leno came to town, as he did for a week's worth of tapings of his late-night TV show in 1996, he picked up the phone and called Eppie and asked for her help.

"What did he want?" I asked.

"He wanted to know if I would get in a car with him and go to strangers' homes, knock on their doors, and ask which way they hang their toilet paper," Eppie said. "He, or maybe one of his staff, must have remembered the toilet-paper column. Do you remember it?"

"Not when it first ran but I read about it in your new book," I said.

"Well," she said. "One of the things Larry [Fanning] told me when I started writing the column was, 'You can deal with any subject as long as you use the right words. But one thing you can't do, you can't take your readers into the bathroom.' Well, twenty-two years later I forgot that." And in 1977, she printed a letter that asked her to settle the matter of which was the correct way to hang toilet paper.

"Do people really care?" I asked.

"They do. They do," Eppie said. "Would you believe fifteen thousand five hundred letters from people who care? I almost hadn't printed the letter in the first place. I thought it was inconsequential. I had no idea how many people cared passionately about toilet paper."

Eppie would address the subject again a number of times throughout the years, and readers by the thousands would again chime in to explain why having the sheets of the toilet paper come "over the top" or "from underneath" was the correct method of hanging the paper. One of the recent revisits to the "tissue issue" is what caught the eye of Leno or his producers.

"So what did you tell Leno?" I asked.

"I said no," Eppie said. "I like Jay. He's a very decent man, but . . ."

It would be impossible to calculate how many offers Eppie declined to do things—endorse products, plug books or political candidates—that might sully the reputation she had built and so steadfastly maintained. Popo had over the years endorsed a number of products, and it infuriated Eppie when some people mistook her sister for her in the ads.

"It's important for people to know that I'm on the level," Eppie said.

New issues were always arising, and Eppie never shied away from addressing them. She wanted to be connected and "on the level" when it came to the important matters confronting or confusing her readers or the country. One of these was AIDS. Her column was arguably the first place many people had ever read about venereal disease, a topic she had been addressing since the 1950s, and the first place, early in 1976, where people learned of what one letter writer called "the latest VD bummer," herpes simplex 2. Eppie also used her column to alert readers to the latest medical advances and other health-related news. And, as early as 1983, AIDS was in her column. She explained the etiology and symptoms of the disease to readers. But perhaps more important, she tried to dispel the myths surrounding the disease, and she was especially eager to help those who had been cut off from family and friends because they had what many in the general population referred to as the "gay plague." To one HIV-positive man who had been forbidden to see his young nieces because of his illness, she wrote, "Your brother and his wife need to be educated."

Educating the readers remained at the forefront, even when it meant publishing provocative letters such as the following.

"Dear Ann Landers:

Last night I had sex with 4,096 people. Impossible, you say? You're wrong.

"I'm a divorced woman who has had a faithful lover for quite some time. Last night I had too much to drink and like a crazy fool I had sex with a man I had seen several times at our tennis club. He admitted having sex with eight 'perfectly respectable' female partners over the last year.

"I worked a chart backward the same as in our tennis seeding. I took those eight women and assumed that they also had slept with eight men each, and each of those eight men had had sex with eight women, etc.

"By using simple arithmetic progression, after only three series I realized that I had been exposed somewhere along the line to 4,096 persons, plus one.

"How can I assume that there was no one in that family tree who was not an AIDS carrier, if only through a blood transfusion? I understand that there are 10,000 carriers in our state alone. How do I know I haven't been 'seeded,' and I don't mean tennis?

"From now on I am sticking to my lover and hope to make him my husband for life. I pray he never will have to pay a price for my having exposed myself to 4,097 people. Sign me . . . —Scared."

During my interview with Eppie about her new book, I asked what it was like to ride the waves of change that had taken her and the column from acne to AIDS, courtship to crack, necking to cross-dressing. "I had never heard about drugs forty years ago, and today so many letters are about drugs and guns and violence," she said. "People are getting tougher and meaner, more suspicious and less trusting. But basically, the problems are the same. The family is where the problems lie and where they always will. But I am confident that the human species will survive. I read the letters and I am amazed. I think to myself, 'What courage. What bravery.' "

It can be a courageous act to publicly change one's mind, especially in front of 90 million people. It's even more courageous to do so continually. Eppie had always strongly advocated acceptance and tolerance of gays but remained adamant that it was a personality disorder. But in 1992, she used her column to announce a significant change in that attitude when she published a letter citing research that had established that genetics played a major role in human sexuality. That mention resulted in one of the largest column responses, nearly eighty thousand letters. Some of them angrily disagreed, but most expressed gratitude that Eppie had raised the issue, and the letter writers expressed themselves with great emotion, a compelling mixture of sorrow and pride.

The *Oprah* crew was still filming in the apartment as my interview was winding down. "Before you go," Eppie said to me, "let's look out the window. I really do think I have the best view in town."

It was May and the weather was warm. People lay on the

sand beach. Others rode bikes and jogged along the concrete path that separated the beach from the eight lanes of traffic on the Outer Drive. Lake Michigan stretched east and north as far as I could see.

"I like this view best at night," Eppie said, "when I can watch the lights of cars sweeping along the drive. I sometimes like to watch boats on the lake, but I have never been fond of the winters. But I'll always argue that it snows more in Wisconsin than Chicago."

"Did you ever think of moving from Chicago?" I asked.

"I was tempted to move to California once, in the early eighties," she said.

"Why didn't you?" I asked.

"I started mentioning the California idea to friends. A few thought it was a good idea. Others thought it was silly. Two of those who didn't want me to go, [former University of Chicago president] Ed Levi and [attorney] Bill Kirby, drew up these 'official legal' papers saying that while it was legally acceptable for Eppie Lederer to work somewhere other than Chicago, she was not free to live there. I laughed so hard I forgot all about California."

We said our good-byes, and as I walked back to the paper, I tried to imagine Eppie living anywhere but Chicago. She was one of ours, and we were proud of it. Perhaps because we don't have as many celebrities as Los Angeles or New York, Chicagoans cling to those we do have with blind chauvinism, even if they were not born here, or no longer live and work here. Oprah's ours. Studs Terkel, too. Michael Jordan's no Bull, but he's still ours. Noble Prize–winning novelist Saul Bellow moved a while

ago, but we still think of him as one of our own. All those actors
who've gone from local storefront theaters to make it big in
movies and TV—John Malkovich, Gary Sinise, William L.
Petersen, Laurie Metcalf—are still firmly tied to Chicago, if
only in our minds.

Later, writing the story about Eppie and her new book,
I called Margo for quotes and she said her mother was "an
American institution. She is America's bulletin board. By read-
ing her, one can keep track of what's going on in the country. . . .
And she really cares about what she does. She's determined to fix
the world or die trying."

The story appeared on the front page of "Tempo." Eppie
called to say that she liked it, and so did most of the paper's top
editors and executives, though the one who had given me the
"be tough" directions, complained, "You weren't mean enough."

A couple of years later, after I had been gratefully relieved of
the "Tempo" editing job and was working as a senior writer on
the staff of the *Tribune Sunday Magazine,* I was walking out of a
boozy good-bye lunch for Gosselin, who was retiring as the
Magazine editor, when he put his arm around me and said,
"You're going to get a call from Eppie."

"What about?" I asked.

Gosselin just smiled, and a few days later I got the call.

"I was wondering, with Dennis leaving, if you might take
over the editing of the column," Eppie said. "I would really be
indebted, and I want you to be tough on me."

"I'm really flattered you'd ask. But I'm not sure I'd be any
good," I said. "I hate to admit it, but I really haven't been a regular reader of your column."

"That's honest," Eppie said, pausing long enough to make me think that she might be trying to figure out a gentle way to say, "Well, then, thanks but no thanks." Instead she said, "Not a regular reader? Well, that's been your mistake. Now you'll have to be one."

14

· LOT 2643 ·

Louis XIV–Style Chinoiserie Decorated and
Parcel Gilt Mirror

E very Monday morning I walked from my desk to the suite of offices on the fifth floor of the *Tribune* and picked up a pile of neatly typed pages. There were only twenty-eight pages of bright yellow paper, but they often seemed heavier than a Sunday *New York Times* because I couldn't help thinking that what was in my hands would appear, in a few weeks, in twelve hundred newspapers and be read by 90 million people.

The four women working in Eppie's outer office were immediately delightful and friendly. I had seen and shared

"Some weather we're having," small talk with them when we found ourselves together on elevator rides. But until the *Tribune* editorial department expanded to the fifth floor of the Tribune Tower, Eppie's suite of offices there provided little opportunity for Eppie's assistants to get to know the rest of the staff.

Kathy Mitchell, Marcy Sugar, Barb Olin, and Catherine Richardson were longtime employees of Eppie's, all of them on her staff for more than a decade. Kathy had been there her entire working life, starting with her as a typist in 1969, when she was nineteen. Few people in the world were closer to Eppie than was Kathy, who held the informal title of personal assistant and office manager, and who would become a trustee of Eppie's will.

When I came in to the office every Monday, I enjoyed grabbing a chair, sitting down, and talking with the women Eppie called "her girls." Lively, smart, and eager for gossip, they also had wonderful stories about Eppie and were fiercely loyal to her.

"Do you know why we asked for a private bathroom when we came over to the *Tribune*?" Kathy asked me rhetorically one day. "At the *Sun-Times,* we didn't have one and one of us had to go with Eppie to the ladies' room because there would usually be some total stranger handing her a piece of paper under the stall door and asking for an autograph. Eppie gracefully obliged, but it happened so often, it was driving us nuts."

Kathy also traveled frequently with Eppie and told me, "She was such a hoot. The first thing she always did was introduce herself to the pilots and flight crew—find out if they were married, dating, how many children they had, what the weather was going to be. She loved spending time in the cockpit before takeoff."

I loved hearing these stories and appreciated the advice the "girls" gave me about the columns. "She really means it when she says she wants you to be tough," said Marcy.

But I went at the columns gently at first, mostly just looking for typographical errors. It was inconceivable to me that I might discover something that would prompt a "Well, you're dead wrong about this advice to 'Lonely in Abilene.' I don't think a twelve-year-old should be dating a guy in his seventies." Immediately—for as I told her I had not been a regular reader—I was impressed with the simplicity of the weekly packages, the lively mix of letters, and how practical and straightforward and direct Eppie's answers were. I went into the *Tribune* morgue, which is what some of us still call the newspaper's library, and checked out and read the few books written about Eppie, looking for definition for the revelations the columns were causing.

Professor David Grossvogel's *Dear Ann Landers*, published in 1987, did provide some insight. Although it reads like a work of scholarship—the Cornell University professor did, after all, read, classify, and analyze thirty years' worth of columns—it does contain many interesting observations and assessments, such as this: "In articulating generally accepted values, Ann Landers is a mirror rather than an analyst. She does not set the standards but finds them in the aspirations of those who write to her. Confirmations of those values comes from the authorities to whom she appeals. . . . She believes that the virtue of plain language matches the precision of moral explicitness. . . . Her voice has a mythical resonance, since it is, for many of her readers, the voice of a social culture."

A couple of months after I started editing the column, I got my first invitation to dinner with Eppie. Although her building was about ten blocks from the *Tribune* offices and it was freezing outside, I walked, in order to freshen up, so to speak; to get rid of, as best I could, the smell of cigarette smoke. I spent a few minutes shaking off the cold, shivering in the ornate lobby of the building, and asking the doorman to wait before calling up and telling Eppie that I was there. She greeted me at the door to her apartment, asking, "How cold is it outside? You look like you're freezing."

Our first few dinners always took place at the International Club in the Drake Hotel, a private club only half a block from Eppie's apartment. Each member had a small golden nameplate on his or her favorite table, food was served with a grand if dusty formality, and the wait staff was solicitous almost to the point of parody.

Though she was steadfast in avoiding liquor herself, she always insisted that I have a drink, or two, often saying, "Larry [Fanning] used to drink, so go ahead, have another one but I don't want you getting schnockered."

"You remind me a lot of Larry," she would often tell me during our subsequent dinners and when I would accompany her to various events. I was pleased by that, knowing how much Eppie had liked and admired Larry. It was more than just the cocktails. I think she saw in me the vestige of the old-fashioned newspapermen with whom she had worked in the early years of her career.

But Eppie was also well aware that I was a child of a different era, a child of the '60s, a baby boomer, and that this generation gap could actually benefit the column. "What I really need is for you to keep me on my toes," Eppie told me. "Anything you don't think sounds right, let me know. Anything you think is out of date, let me know. And don't hesitate to disagree with me if you think my answer if off base or dead wrong."

At first I thought this ridiculous: Meryl Streep telling a film director to "Watch out in case I drool while I'm saying my lines"; Tiger Woods saying, "Tell me if I'm hitting these nine irons too close to the hole"; Mother Nature saying, "Let me know if that sky's too blue."

But I soon realized that even as she closed in on eighty, Eppie was still determined to not just keep working but to keep providing her readers with a contemporary column filled with up-to-date issues. "That's so important to me," she said. "I plan to die at my typewriter."

"That's the way we all should go," I said.

During that first dinner we talked a lot about Margo. "She's writing again," Eppie said. "Doing a column for a magazine in Boston. It's very good."

I had certainly known the details of Margo's life while she lived in Chicago, knew that Margo's marriage to John Coleman had dissolved in 1967, and that during the couple's five years of marriage, they had three children: Abra (named for Eppie's father, Abraham), Adam, and Andrea Ted, who would always be better known as Cricket.

After her divorce from Coleman, Margo fell into a writing career when she charmed *Chicago Tribune* film critic Gene Siskel, with whom she shared a table at the wedding reception of a mutual friend. Siskel introduced her to editors at the *Tribune*. Her first published story was a three-thousand-word account of what it was like to be a Playboy bunny for three days. She was soon writing a column two days a week for the *Tribune*. Six months later it was picked up for national syndication. "When I became a syndicated columnist and people figured out the connection with the old lady, I had offers from a lot of women's magazines and one of the news magazines to do an advice column," Margo would later tell me. "I always said no."

In 1972, she also said no to writing when she married Jules Furth, a good-looking, athletically built Chicago funeral director, whom Eppie and Jules liked considerably more than Coleman. When that marriage ended in 1976, Margo returned to writing, as a features reporter for the *Chicago Daily News*. Perhaps it was this move, seemingly toward careerism, that prompted Eppie to ask Margo if she eventually wanted to take over the "Ann Landers" column. "Not me, honey," said Margo. "I don't want to work that hard."

Margo's feature stories at the *Daily News* often included celebrity interviews, and in December 1976, she sat down at a table to have a luncheon interview with actor Ken Howard, who was in Chicago appearing onstage as the star of *Equus*. Within four months, Margo became Mrs. Ken Howard in a ceremony that took place at the Art Institute of Chicago.

Eppie liked Ken Howard, calling the six-foot, six-inch actor "The Gorgeous Goy . . . a marvelous guy, solid, a real mensch." Her attitudes concerning interfaith marriages had relaxed over the years. And Margo's marriage to Howard helped solidify her change in attitude: Find the right person and worship how you want.

In 1977, Margo, Howard, and her three children moved to

California. The next year he launched his hit television series, *The White Shadow*. They were divorced in 1993, and Margo moved to Cambridge, Massachusetts, outside Boston.

Eppie and I rarely talked much about her grandchildren, though she was obviously fond and proud of them and her great-grandchildren. She was far more interested in discussing people we knew, such as my mother ("She was very beautiful when she was younger. How does she look?"), and people she knew ("Now, that Al Gore is a really fine person but he needs to show his true personality").

She was a great storyteller and if her stories often featured world-famous people, there was never anything pretentious about it. She would mention people such as Princess Diana, Barbara Walters, and Oprah Winfrey in the same easy manner in which you might mention the names of those in your bowling league or bridge club.

At this and other dinners, we talked about the women in my life but never about the men in hers. I didn't think that was any of my business. I still don't. I saw no scandal, nothing titillating about an attractive single woman in her late seventies going on dates with men or even having sex. I knew some of the men with whom Eppie kept company and knew that some of them were younger. But so what? At that age what's a decade in age difference? Besides, if the choice was younger or older, what would you do? But she must have been a great date, for whenever we were together she had an endearingly coquettish way of focusing all of her attention on my life, which included, during our time together, a divorce and remarriage.

She was so supportive during the divorce, and afterward

would tell me, "You are too old to be on the loose. You've got to find a good person to settle down with. So who are these people you're dating? When you get serious about one, you'll have to let me meet her. I'll need to check her out and approve her."

Her hearing was weak in one ear, but she masked it well. She had what I like to think of as a quiet vanity, one that compelled her to wear high heels even if she had begun to walk gingerly. She never broadcast any surgical enhancements in which she may have indulged, but she was not reluctant to talk about it, from the rhinoplasty performed when she was a young bride to, in her later years, touting to her friends and sister Popo the joys of Botox. Her "enhancements," combined with a lifetime of no booze or cigarettes, and a rigorous daily exercise routine that including stretching and climbing up and down the back stairs of her building, made her look a dozen years younger than she was. She was justifiably proud of her figure, often saying, "I still fit in dresses I've had for years." She never ate very much, usually just a couple of appetizers, and she loved dessert, particularly those that included chocolate. Whenever she did order an entrée, there was food left over, and she insisted that it be wrapped and would tote it home and stick it in the refrigerator.

"I'll admit, I'm not much of a cook," she said.

Around the time I started editing Eppie's column, I also began writing a weekly feature for the *Tribune Sunday Magazine* called "Sidewalks." Each week photographer Charles Osgood and I get into his messy car and just start driving, not looking for anything special, though we expect to find special things and people. We do this not because we are looking for big messages, but because we want to explore every corner of this place we call home. "Sidewalks" brings us into contact with people and places and things that quietly share and shape the Chicago area. These are not the sorts of characters or sites or items that make, or even deserve to make, front-page news. Their stories are less solo performances than part of the ongoing city symphony.

Eppie would often send me notes about the column, about the people and places we encountered. This was one of her most endearing habits, sending handwritten notes to reporters about stories that she admired. Whenever I got one of these I felt like a kid who had gotten a "Good going" from his teacher. "Such a wonderful story and great man," she wrote about a "Sidewalks" column that featured a man who sold peanuts on the exit ramp of the Eisenhower Expressway on the city's tough West Side. "That these kinds of hardworking people are out there gives me great hope for the city." Another note, about some kids playing in a park in an otherwise down-at-the-heels section of the South Side, said, "You made me feel like I should go visit this beautiful park."

The people and places in "Sidewalks" were not the sort of people and places Eppie knew personally. But these were people she knew intimately through their letters. Hers was a rarefied place. But in reading her columns each week, I became convinced that somehow, even though her life provided a comforting armor of sorts against the hundreds of troubles she encountered every day, this sort of isolation enabled her to deal with problems more objectively than might one who had a bunch of his or her own.

Her responses were never very long, but they were precise: Dump the loser, mind your own business, get a pet, wake up and smell the coffee. She did not lecture or pontificate. She sometimes barely wrote more than a couple of sentences in a response. It was obvious that for her, the column was a collaborative effort. By giving her readers a voice, she was allowing a louder, collective voice to be heard. She did not get up on a soapbox. Rather, in the most selfless and effective way, she allowed herself to be the soapbox. The voices in her column were mostly those of so-called ordinary folks—the same as the "Sidewalks" people—but as they spoke, other ordinary folks read and listened and understood and acted. It was true that millions looked to her for guidance, but few realized the subtle ways in which she was providing it.

Editing the column was not difficult. Some weeks it was hard to find even a minor typographical error. It was also something of a nostalgic kick to edit with a pencil on paper, many newspapers having become all-computer edited more than twenty years earlier.

Since each week's pile of yellow pages was accompanied by a Post-it note with a handwritten message from Eppie saying, "Hope this works" or "Not sure about this week; be tough" I started responding in kind, tagging the pages with my own notes: "How about changing the reference here from The Beatles to U2?" I began doing Internet searches on some of the poems readers sent in, to make sure of their authorship. I would search the *Tribune*'s archives to find stories that might help her embellish the information in a response. I would write "Great letter" and compliment her with a "Good, tough response" when she unloaded on a reader. She seemed pleased, as she would tell me through phone calls, at our occasional dinners, and in the weekly notes that came with new batches of columns. I was pleased, too, which is why one day in May 2000, I asked her if we could go to dinner somewhere other than the International Club.

"Where would we go?" she asked, sounding a bit surprised but enthusiastic. "One of the hip new places?"

"If that's what you'd like," I said.

"I'll get really dolled up," she said.

It wasn't so much that I had tired of the International Club. How could anyone tire of the room's clubby atmosphere and gentlemanly wait staff, or its food and drinks, which were tasty and ample, respectively? But by this time I was feeling guilty about accepting dinners on Eppie, even though she argued, "It's the only way I have to pay you back for the editing."

After a couple of years editing her column, I was convinced that I was getting more out of our relationship than she was. In the weekly letters I was reading, I was learning a great deal about people and problems that were not a part of my world. People wrote to Ann Landers about problems that have vexed human beings for centuries: sex (not enough, too much, too strange); troublesome relatives, specifically in-laws, who dropped in too often, stayed too long, tried to dictate how to raise children, make a bed, fold a towel; money, the lack of it, primarily, though a few lottery winners wrote wondering what to do with too much of it; kids, from dealing with the girl who refused to stop eating candy bars to the teenager who wanted a tattoo. The only "new" problems were about computers, primarily about spouses who spent too much time on the machines, causing suspicions of Internet hanky-panky. Through the letters that Eppie ran, I believed that I was gaining a better perspective on this country, the pressures and troubles felt by those in small towns and suburbs.

Around this time I met, and later wrote about, a man picking through a garbage can in an alley. He did not want to talk, did not want to tell me his name, did not want to even tell me what he was doing, though it was obvious from the items he had in a large bag—pieces of scrap metal and cans—that he was looking for things he might sell later. However hard his life might have been, there was a certain pride in the way he brushed me off, saying, "Leave me alone, now. I'm not bothering you or anybody that I know of. I'm just out here trying to get by. Now get away and let me do my work."

I left him alone, but within a couple of blocks I thought for the first time in a long time about how simple and low-tech so many lives remain; how the problems in those lives revolve around basic issues, the basic issues of life that filled Eppie's columns. Meeting people like that man in the alley, or the waitress at the corner diner, the guy bagging groceries, the cop on a horse, the construction worker hauling bricks, or the man or woman cutting your hair, reminds me that there is an honesty and dignity in what too many of us might now deem "old-fashioned" work, "ordinary" lives, "commonplace" problems.

When I would read some of the columns' letters, I tried to imagine what the writers and the people they were writing about looked like, where they lived. I would often make movies in my head and, thanks to Eppie, they all had happy endings.

I had started trying to pick up the tab at the International Club, but that was never possible; at such an establishment members are sent a monthly accounting in a discreet white envelope. I became determined to try to repay Eppie for the new and refreshing perspective her columns were giving me. I called my old friend, Demetri Alexander, who owned the State Room, one of Chicago's hottest new restaurants at the time. I asked him if we could get a table without waiting and he said, "Oh, my God. Ann Landers. I love her. I met her thirty years ago at a party at the Palmer House and I've never forgotten. I read her every day. She's a legend. Is she nice?"

"What do you think?" I asked.

"Well, of course, she would be wonderful," said Demetri. "What time?"

I picked Eppie up at her apartment and we took a cab the six blocks to the restaurant where Demetri was waiting, standing behind the host stand.

"Miss Landers," said Demetri. "What a pleasure to see you again. You won't remember, but I met you at a party at the Drake in 1971 and you—"

"And you remember that?" Eppie said.

"Who could forget meeting you, Miss Landers?" he said.

"How sweet," she said. She was always genuinely flattered when people would recognize or remember her.

Demetri—"He's a nice young fellow," Eppie whispered— led us through the dining area which was a bilevel space of white-clothed tables against plush white banquettes. When seated we looked out across the expanse of the main dining room, surveying the action. "This is quite a place," said Eppie. "Now this Demetri, what's his background?"

I told her about Demetri and ordered a drink. We had just

begun looking over the menu when Demetri appeared with a woman on his arm. Or someone who appeared to be a woman. I recognized Chili Pepper immediately and made the introductions. Chili, who will speak with a thick accent when the mood strikes her, said, "What a pleasure it is to meet you," and Eppie, assuming that Chili was Spanish or Mexican, began to speak in Spanish.

"You are Spanish?" asked Chili.

"No, dear," Eppie said. "I'm Jewish."

"You speak so well," said Chili. "Most people make mistakes. Sometimes people mistake me for a woman."

"You're, you're not a woman?" said Eppie. She seemed visibly shocked and, putting her hand under the table, banged my knee.

"No, darling, I am a man," said Chili.

Eppie banged my leg again.

"Chili's the most famous and best female impersonator in Chicago," I said.

I started talking with Demetri about business, and Eppie began an animated conversation with Chili. A few minutes later, when I heard Eppie say, "Friedman. I was born Esther Pauline Friedman and then became Mrs. Jules Lederer," I turned away from Demetri.

"What are you two talking about?" I asked.

Eppie said, "Chili here was asking about my name."

"And your husband, Ann?" Chili asked.

"You can call me Eppie. All of my friends call me Eppie," she said.

"And your husband, Eppie, he—" Chili asked.

"He was just the greatest salesman," Eppie said.

"And what did he sell?" asked Chili.

"He could sell anything," said Eppie.

Among Jules Lederer's many sales jobs was selling pots and pans door to door. He had, in the 1940s, the then-innovative notion of throwing demonstration dinners in peoples' homes, and Eppie went along. "I was his dishwasher," she said. "I listened in the kitchen as he racked up the sales in the living room."

"You washed the dishes?" said Demetri, laughing. "Maybe I could use you here."

"I could still do it," Eppie said.

"I'll bet you could," said Demetri.

Demetri left the table, Chili and Eppie kept talking, and I sat back and sipped my drink, thinking what a wonderfully odd encounter I was witnessing: this seemingly square eighty-year-old, with her perfect bouffant and her teetotaling ways, engaged in animated conversation with Chicago's leading female impersonator. This was just another example, I thought, of how open Eppie was to people, how tolerant of (and curious about) what many might deem "alternative" lifestyles. We would never have dinner again at the International Club after that night at the State Room. "What's the hot new place and when's our next dinner?" Eppie would ask, and we would make plans and then visit new restaurants, and she would always get "dolled up."

That night at the State Room, Eppie laughed, grabbed my arm, and said, "Chili has invited us to come and see her perform some night. It's a club, the Baton. Won't that be fun?" She turned back to Chili and said: "Now tell me more about your life. It must be very unusual. Much more interesting than mine."

· LOT 1275C ·

IBM Selectric III Typewriter

The first time Eppie and I talked about death was in April 1997. I was not yet editing Eppie's column, but I was writing Mike Royko's obituary. He had been stricken with an aneurysm at his suburban Winnetka home and rushed to Northwestern Memorial Hospital in downtown Chicago, about midway between Eppie's apartment building and Tribune Tower. It took him nearly a week, fighting futilely, to die, and every day during that time Eppie would call me—knowing that I was Mike's friend, but also because she knew I was in contact with the hospital and members of Mike's family—and ask, "Is there any hope?" The other person to call every day was Jimmy Breslin, the New York columnist. He asked about Mike, and he also asked about Eppie, because, as he said, "We're the last of the old breed."

"Have you seen him?" Eppie asked, referring to Mike.

"I did. It wasn't pretty," I said. "[Mike's wife] Judy let me come over to the hospital, and I spent a few minutes alone with him in his room."

"Did he know you were there?"

"No."

"Are you okay? I know you don't handle death well at all."

"I'm sort of okay," I said, remembering how she had offered me the names and numbers of two psychiatrists and the suggestion that I call them after hearing me speak at my father's memorial service almost a decade before.

I suppose that when you reach a certain age—what might it be, eighty?—death becomes such a familiar part of your life that it is not something you turn away from, even as it mirrors your own mortality. Eppie's later years were filled with funerals, as friends and acquaintances died with chilling regularity. Her own parents had died relatively young, her mother in 1944 at fifty-six and her father nine years later at sixty-four. Mike was only sixty-four.

During the days Mike was dying she sent me a note: "No one likes to think about dying, but occasionally we need to remember life's limitations. In the midst of tragedy, my readers find the time to educate me about the best ways to face this ultimate challenge."

I don't know if that is something she had previously written or if it was from some other writer. She printed so many letters about death over the years, often directing people to grief-counseling organizations, sometimes lighter in tone, but all of them reflecting her philosophy that dying should be done with dignity.

Eppie told me this story during the week Mike was dying: "It was last November. I was at home, in my nightgown, when the phone rang. It was Ken Velo [executive assistant to Chicago's Cardinal Joseph Bernardin]. He said that Joe wanted to see me. Joe was dying. Pancreatic cancer, and I knew the end was near. Joe had been getting calls from all sorts of friends. Clinton called. The pope called. So Ken tells me Joe wants to see me and that he'll send a car, and I put on a robe and a coat and go over to the mansion. I got there and Joe was sleeping. I said, 'Joe, it's Eppie. Can you hear me?' He nodded. And I said, 'Don't try to talk. We'll just sit here and pray, me to my God and you to yours.' It's really the same God. So I just sat there and talked to him and held his hand. I really think he heard me. He died that day. I will always be glad I was there."

She was there a few years later, too, standing with me outside a synagogue in Highland Park, a Chicago suburb, after the funeral service for *Tribune* film critic Gene Siskel. The previous Saturday I had written Siskel's obituary, which ran on the front page of the Sunday *Tribune*. Many of us at the paper had known that Gene was sick, that for ten months he had been waging a strenuous and relatively quiet battle against complications that arose after the removal of a growth from his brain. That battle ended on February 20, 2000, when the fifty-three-year-old critic died.

Obituaries are among the most common elements of newspapers. Their length and placement in the paper is commensurate, at least in some editors' minds, with the fame, celebrity, importance, or influence of the person who has died. The coverage of funerals and memorial services by newspapers is less common. But Siskel was a national celebrity, thanks in large part to his long-running TV show with *Sun-Times* critic Roger Ebert, and he was one of the *Tribune*'s own, and so, notebook in hand, there I was on that sun-splashed Monday, talking to people walking out of the funeral.

Siskel had been given a simple and muted memorial service in front of more than fifteen hundred family members, colleagues, admirers, and friends. Those in attendance who had expected a parade of high-profile eulogists were disappointed. The memorial duties were left solely to a rabbi, who admitted that his task was "daunting." He said his intention was to celebrate Siskel "not as a public personality but as a member of a family." But many yearned for more. As the large crowd dispersed, I heard the sort of critical remarks for which Siskel was so justifiably famous. Many of the people at the funeral were, after all, the sort not loath to offer opinions, and they rated the service as they might have a movie.

Eppie walked up to me and whispered, "You'll tell it like it was, won't you?"

"What do you mean?" I asked.

"That was terrible," she said. "That man didn't know Gene very well."

I went back to the paper to write the story for the next day's editions, and during the couple of hours it took to do so, Eppie called four times, each time more adamant about telling it "like it was." On some level I knew she was right. I decided to quote her but not use her name, lest some of Gene's relatives call her to complain. She didn't need that hassle. I wrote: " 'I felt that the rabbi talked too much about himself,' said one prominent

columnist. 'There was no passion, and his words did not cap-
ture the Gene most people knew.' "

We took a lot of heat from one or two angry relatives and editors who complained to me because my name was on the story,
and to Eppie because people surmised her identity. The paper
even ran this "correction": "A report Tuesday on the memorial service for *Tribune* movie columnist Gene Siskel contained an inappropriate characterization of the eulogy delivered by Rabbi
Vernon Kurtz of North Suburban Synagogue Beth El. The *Tribune*
regrets the error." But Eppie called me and said, "I'm proud of
you, and I think Gene would have been too. You don't really get a
chance to control things after you're gone, and that's too bad."

Eppie did have a chance at some control. Her obituary, or a
rough version of it, was already written. Just a few months before
Siskel's funeral, veteran reporter Jon Anderson was assigned to
write it. He called her and explained what he was doing. Eppie
invited him over. I told her later I thought this was kind of creepy,
though it is a common practice at newspapers to write obituaries
of notable people when they reach a certain age or seem vulnera-
ble to illness or accident. Editors are the worrying kind.

"It's not creepy. It's the newspaper business," Eppie told
me. "And this way I get to make sure there's nothing in there
that's wrong. And look, everybody has to have an obituary.
When you get one that's written by a person you knew, it's kind
of like a good-bye letter."

When Anderson finished his obituary on Eppie, he sent it to
her with a note: "Dear Eppie, Here's a first draft. Could you let
me know if any names or facts are wrong? Hope we never have
to run it. Thanks, Jon."

She sent it back to him a few days later with a handwritten note. Actually there were two notes. The first thanked Jon and noted "very few people get the privilege of fact-checking their own obituary." Under that note was another, with an arrow pointing to a circle that Eppie had made around a small stain on the paper with the words "spaghetti stain." Eppie didn't make many changes to the copy, but she made a few, clarifying some language, correcting the color of her limousine from "black" to "navy blue."

The most extensive changes were to a couple of sentences that read, "In a 1982 incident, she was caught recycling letters. 'Let's just say it wasn't my finest hour,' she noted, begging her readers for their forgiveness."

Eppie edited this to read, "In 1982, she used some letters that had been published previously. 'Let's just say it wasn't my finest hour,' she said in an apology."

Emphasizing the importance of the last change was a note from Kathy Mitchell: "If possible, Eppie would love if you took the recycling reference out."

The "recycling reference" had to do with one of the most potentially damaging incidents in her career. Though Eppie was usually able to effectively mute criticism by giving herself in print "forty lashes with a wet noodle," things were not so easily remedied when it was discovered in 1982 that one of her columns had featured a "recycled" letter. A reporter spent weeks going through microfilm at the Chicago Public Library and found that a number of the same letters and responses had appeared frequently over the years.

The reporter who had detailed the recycling thought Eppie handled the situation in an "admirable way." Most people did not consider this an ethical breach but rather a result of expedience brought about by the brutal seven-day-a-week schedule, though most thought she should have labeled the letters "previously published." *Sun-Times* editor Jim Hoge told Eppie, "Come clean, get it behind you, and move on. I didn't have to say, 'Don't ever do it again.'"

She never did. But in 1995 she created an even bigger stir, not in print as Ann Landers but as Eppie Lederer. During an interview with *New Yorker* writer Christopher Buckley, she was asked about some of the people she knew. Though typically blunt about some—(Geraldo Rivera "is so trashy," Ronald Reagan "is a sweet guy. You know, he's totally gone. I had a letter from Nancy just a few weeks ago, and she said, 'I feel like half a person'")—her response about Pope John Paul II was incendiary: "His eyes are sky blue, his cheeks are pink and adorable-looking, and he has a sweet sense of humor . . . Of course, he's a Polack . . . They're very antiwomen."

Once the magazine hit newsstands and mailboxes, criticism from readers and several Polish-American groups was swift. "People are outraged," said Edward Dykla, president of the Polish Roman Catholic Union of America. "They want action. For a person of her stature and visibility to say something like that is completely uncalled for, unprofessional."

Veteran Chicago broadcaster Sig Sakowicz, then media director of the Polish National Alliance, said his office was deluged with complaints. "I thought she knew better," said Sakowicz.

"You don't make these stupid remarks. She's not only flagrantly talking down the pope but Polish men and all Poles as well. It's a trifecta."

Eppie issued a statement of apology immediately. But the wet noodle wasn't enough this time. The outcry continued. To her rescue came her old pal Mike Royko, whose phone was ringing like crazy. His response—which Eppie told me later was "something that I read over and over"—was in the form of a column. It went like this:

"An old pal from the Northwest Side called and sounded like he might pop a blood vessel.

" 'Are you going to do something about that . . . that . . . woman?' he sputtered.

"What woman?

" 'That Ann Landers woman. Are you going to let her have a blast?'

"Of course not. Ann Landers, also known as Eppie Lederer, has been a close friend for more than 30 years. I don't go around blasting close friends. Especially when they are as cute as a bug.

" 'But you know what she did? What she said?'

"Of course I know.

" 'She called the pope a Polack. A POLACK!'

"So what? The pope is a Polack.

" 'What? What? You said the pope is a Polack? You said it?'

"Of course I said it. And if you ask the pope if he is a Polack, I'm sure he would agree.

" 'I can't believe this. You're part Polish and you can use a slur like that?'

"What slur?

" 'What do you think? The word *Polack.*'

"I don't consider it a slur, and I'm surprised that so many Polacks and others think it is. They have been calling this paper and howling for a sweet lady's scalp.

"So once and for all, let us get it straight. If you are truly Polish, you are a Polack.

"Who says so? The Polish language says so. In Poland, the word for someone who is Polish is Polack.

"Thus, when Eppie, as we call her, described the pope as a Polack, she was 100 percent correct.

"If you went in a bar in Warsaw, hoisted a vodka and said: 'Here's to the pope, a really great Polack,' you would get cheerful nods, especially if you bought the round. Except from the unreconstructed godless commies, the rats.

"That's why I've never understood someone being offended by a perfectly valid word.

"It's not like calling an Italian a wop or a ginzo, a German a kraut or a heinie, a Frenchman a frog, a Hispanic a beaner, or other words that were created as slurs by old WASPs and rival ethnic groups.

"This was explained to me at an early age by Big Chester, who used to tend bar at my father's tavern and was the toughest guy I've ever known.

"Big Chester was born in Poland, and he would thump his chest, fix Irish Harry with a steely gaze and say: 'Oldest university in Europe is in Krakow. We have university when Irish wore fur underwear. We conquer most of Russia when Irish wore fur underwear. I am Polack and proud of it. You want to fight?'

"Irish Harry, who hoped to live long enough to become an

alderman, would just smile weakly and buy the house a round.

"But let us return to my friend Eppie.

"Most of the angry people who called hadn't read the article in the *New Yorker* that caused this flap.

"They had heard it on radio and TV, as reported by bubble-headed broadcast boobs who hadn't read it either.

"So let's get to it.

"In the article, which was about what a great babe Eppie is—and she truly is—she was giving insightful thumbnail impressions of the many famous people she has met. And she has met more of them than anyone but Kup.

"About Pope John Paul II, the Polish pope, she said: 'Looks like an angel. He has the face of an angel. His eyes are sky blue, and his cheeks are pink and adorable looking, and he has a sweet sense of humor.'

"Now, I ask you, did any of the TV yahoos and radio babblers tell you about Eppie saying that the pope looks like an angel and has a sweet sense of humor?

"Of course not. The broadcast rodents knew that would not serve their malicious purpose.

"They zeroed in on the rest of her quote: 'Of course, he's a Polack.' Laughter. 'They're very antiwomen.'

"What she obviously meant was that Poles of the pope's generation don't always treat women as equals. And she's right. There are countless Catholic women—Polish and otherwise, nuns and housewives—who will tell you they aren't nuts about this Polish pope's attitudes toward women.

"And that is a valid issue that can be debated. But it is not a blanket insult of all Polacks.

"So I would ask my fellow Polacks to calm down. This lady ain't got a bigoted bone in her trim bod. And when life gets tough, you couldn't ask for a better friend.

"That's from one proud Polack to another."

The furor was such that Eppie's pope comment became fodder for a "Top 10 List" devoted to a frivolous collection of "Other Ann Landers Mistakes" on *The Late Show with David Letterman*.

10. Frequently refers to Mother Teresa as "that public relations machine"

9. Three years ago gave bad advice to someone called "Miserable at NBC"

8. Told "Scot-Free in Brentwood" to "play a lot of golf while pretending to look for the real killers"

7. Advised the Menendez brothers to "confront" their parents

6. Eating huge plate of buffalo wings before bed

5. Advised "Stuck with a Snoring Husband" to "suffocate the bastard"

4. Referred "Depressed in Detroit" to Dr. Kevorkian

3. Told "Chubby in Washington" to chase those blues away by sending troops to Bosnia

2. Misspelled the word *Polack*

1. The big spread in *Playboy*

Eventually, and after another, lengthier in-print apology from Eppie, things died down. But Mike's coming to her defense was something that profoundly moved Eppie. She always called him "my stand-up guy." So it wasn't surprising to see her walk into the Harold Washington Library at the south edge of downtown Chicago on April 28, 1999.

That was the setting for a celebration of the publication of *One More Time: The Best of Mike Royko,* a collection of Mike's columns. But it was apparent that it was turning into something else, an impromptu memorial service for the famed columnist who had died two years earlier. Though the library's auditorium seated four hundred people and the doors were not due to open until 5 P.M., by noon more than five hundred were lined up around the block waiting to enter. The library staff hustled all afternoon to set up chairs and TVs in other meeting rooms to accommodate the crowd, which eventually would reach nearly one thousand.

Mike's friend, author Studs Terkel, was the master of ceremonies at the library event. He welcomed the audience without benefit of notes: "Seeing your faces, and not a yuppie in the house. What I do see are Mike's people. Look at you. You're working people. You're Chicago. Wrinkled, a cane or two, a walker or two. You're the ones Mike celebrated through the years, you who created the city, the noncelebrated you. Old-time schoolmarms taught us about the 3 Rs, reading, 'riting and 'rithmetic. In Chicago we had our own 3 Rs, Reading Royko as Ritual." He then introduced the speakers.

Nine people were scheduled to speak, including Studs—a collection of Mike's friends, colleagues, and admirers. I was to speak third and was going over my notes when I saw Eppie slide into a seat at the far end of the row. She wasn't scheduled to speak, but it wouldn't have been unusual for her to have a VIP seat.

Mike's friend and colleague, and one of the editors of the collection, Lois Wille, spoke first. She was followed by TV anchor Carol Marin. Then I spoke. As I passed Eppie on my way back to my seat, she grabbed my hand and whispered, "I'm speaking after Mary Schmich. Come over and walk me to the stage."

As *Tribune* columnist Schmich left the stage, I walked over to Eppie, gave her my arm, and together we walked toward the stage. "Wish me luck," she said, as Studs said to the crowd: "Now, Mike, as you know, is a Chicago icon. There's another Chicago icon, and I think together these two columnists have an audience that probably spans the world. I'm referring, of course, to Ann Landers, the one and only, and remember she always advises us . . . those who read her—and a great many millions do—to wake up and smell the coffee, and here then is Ann Landers with reflections on Mike."

The applause started as Eppie made her way from the side of the stage to the podium. Studs said, "Here she comes in all her glory." He hugged her, said, "You're a winner."

Eppie was dressed in a black suit and high heels. She wore a glimmering necklace and earrings. A pin sparkled on her left shoulder. She adjusted the microphone and began: "Everyone on this program tonight was invited to speak. I did not wait for an invitation."

Laughter interrupted her.

She spoke for only a few minutes, calling Mike a genius and

one of the most sophisticated writers of our time. She ended her talk by recalling a party that she and Royko attended. Mike walked over to Eppie and said, "You know, I like your stuff, and you're a good-looking broad."

Eppie paused after that line and again laughter came from the audience. "Well, I can tell you," she said, "that is the best compliment I have ever received in my entire life. Thank you."

16

· LOT 2694 ·

Newspaper from the Day of
Ann Landers's Birth

T he call came late on Saturday afternoon June 22, 2002.
Actually, it was my pager telling me the *Tribune*'s city
desk was trying to reach me. This has never been good
news. It usually means someone has died and I'm being called
to come in to write an obituary. Dialing the phone, a number of
names ran through my mind as I wondered which of them
might no longer be alive.

"Ann Landers just died," said an editor. "We've already got
[Jon] Anderson's obit, but maybe there's something you want
to add or somebody you think we should call."

"I'll get back to you," I said.

My wife, Colleen, came into the room as I was hanging up the phone and said, "Who is it?" "Eppie," I said, almost choking on the name. Though Colleen had not known Eppie long, we both burst into tears and for minutes we just stood there crying.

I called Kathy Mitchell, saying just, "It's Rick." She was crying. "Poor Eppie," she said. "I've got to get over to her apartment." Kathy knew it was coming, but few others did. Eppie had kept her illness a secret to all but a small handful of friends and colleagues and relatives. "She didn't want me to be the one to tell you how sick she was," Kathy said. "She said you had such a hard time with death. She knew you'd just be a basket case."

Eppie's back had begun bothering her near the end of 2001. After an examination in January 2002 at Loyola University Medical Center, doctors told her she had myeloma of the spine, a fatal cancer of the bone marrow. The only question was "When?" Aggressive chemotherapy treatments might mean two more years. Doing nothing might mean a few more months. Eppie chose that latter road and so her life wound down. She had some friends over for tea in February. She went out to dinner in April. She got all dressed up when Father Hesburgh came to visit and when Bill Clinton stopped by in late April.

"She was taking morphine to ease the pain but she always tried to pretend she was feeling okay," said Kathy, who visited the apartment often.

Eppie had her assistants tell everyone who asked that she was having back problems and hoped to be back on her feet soon. Even Eppie was living that lie with some people. It was what she told the woman who had been brought in to care for her.

Still, Eppie kept writing, propped up in bed. Every Monday I picked up the column and read notes she wrote to me, and I edited the column and wrote notes to back to her. One day in April I ran into her driver and aide, Bobby West, a fine and quiet man, in the hallway outside Eppie's office and I told him to give her a hug and tell her it was from me. The next week he said he had done it and she had giggled. He had tears in his eyes. That's when I began to realize how sick Eppie really was.

The invitations to my May 18 wedding had gone out five weeks before, and the first response came from Eppie. I was happy to see a handwritten note on her personalized stationery. It was dated April 17, 2002, and she wrote that if "the hitch in my gitalong gets better, I'll be there! Love, Eppie." A week later, the first gift to arrive was also from Eppie, a beautiful glass pitcher from Tiffany's. There was a note with the gift, and I was disturbed to see that it was printed and not handwritten. That was not like Eppie at all. It wished us "a lifetime of happiness." That's when I knew she wouldn't be at the wedding, when I knew things were bad. I made sure our thank-you note was attached to the next week's batch of columns. I wanted to be sure Eppie knew how much we appreciated her thinking of us.

Eppie was adamant that people stop visiting her. She did not want anyone to see her suffer in the final days. Her granddaughter, Abra, flew in from Minneapolis, arriving on a Saturday; on Eppie's orders, she was denied entrance to the building. Eppie died later that day. The only person with her, at her bedside, was her nurse. She grabbed the nurse's arm, the nurse would later tell a writer for *Chicago* magazine, and then she was gone. The nurse called Kathy, who went to the apartment and started taking care of the details that always follow death.

"It wasn't painful for her," Kathy would tell me. "She was mostly sleeping during the final days, and I like to think that she just went to sleep that last time and didn't get up."

The obituary ran on the front page of the *Tribune* on Sunday, June 23, as did others in most of the country's newspapers and in a number of those in foreign countries.

I had gone into the office on Saturday after getting the sad phone call and did what I could to help put the final obituary together, suggesting the names of people to call for comment, checking some of the facts in the obit. I was even asked to offer some words of my own and they appeared in the obituary: " 'I look for letters that teach something. Or that people can relate to. Or that are very offbeat,' Lederer explained, when asked how she picked from among the 2,000 letters delivered daily to her office on the fifth floor of the Tribune building at 435 N. Michigan Ave.

"The result was a telling and important body of work, said Rick Kogan, her editor for the last five years.

" 'I think that 200 years from now, if an anthropologist really wants to know what life in these United States—all of these United States—was like, all he or she might have to do is read every one of Ann Landers' columns,' Kogan said."

On Monday, radio talk shows were busy with callers expressing their grief. Newspaper columnists offered anecdotes and words of praise.

"She really didn't want anybody to know," said Kathy. "She didn't want to bother anybody, to make them worry."

I imagined what might have happened if people had known. What if she had announced her impending death in her column? Would the sidewalk of East Lake Shore Drive in front of her apartment building have been packed with strangers carrying all sorts of home remedies, flowers, cards, and teddy bears? Would the lobby of her building have been jammed with reporters and camera crews trying to figure out how to sneak upstairs? What would I have done?

I spent a lot of time in Eppie's office the Monday after she died, trading stories with Kathy, Marcy Sugar, Barb Olin, and Catherine Richardson. I could feel their loss, hear it in their voices. Eventually (I had been purposely putting it off), I picked up the pile of twenty-eight pages of yellow paper that was sitting in its familiar spot on top of a filing cabinet. "So this is it?" I asked and Kathy nodded. These columns would not appear for a month, the last one scheduled to run on July 27. I tucked the sheaf into my briefcase. I wasn't going to read it until the weekend. That's the way we used to work it and I saw no reason to change now. Anyway, I had other things to read, the first of which was Margo's column, which ran in newspapers on June 24 and was a tender farewell to readers on her mom's behalf.

Margo was no stranger to writing columns. After she moved to Boston in 1993, she spent three years writing the monthly "Lunch on the Left Bank" column for *Boston* magazine but stopped after a change of ownership at the magazine. That's when her old friend, former *New Republic* editor Michael Kinsley, asked if she would take over the "Dear Prudence" column that was part of the online *Slate* magazine he founded and edited. Its original writer was calling it quits after a year.

204 · Rick Kogan

The columns came easily to her and so did an interesting revelation: "For more than thirty years I said no to advice because it didn't interest me," Margo told me. "But once I started writing the column, I was shocked that it came so easily. I said to the old lady, 'Do you think there's an advice gene?' "

She said Eppie told her, "I don't really think there is. But you were raised around it. If you're awake, you can't help but learn from what's going on around you." Eppie became an avid reader of her daughter's column, which Margo would print out each week and fax to her mom. "I think she gives really good advice," Eppie told me. "She's so cutting edge. She's more liberal in her attitudes than I am, but she's always had her own way of thinking, her own way of doing things."

"Dear Prudence" was vastly different from Eppie's column, and Margo saw it mainly as an interesting diversion rather than a life's calling. "I have had to seek Mother's advice over the years and she's been very good about it," Margo said. "I am proud of her. She's made a real contribution. But for me she's sort of an anti–role model. I do not have her work ethic or her sense of service. I never wanted to knock myself out. I wanted to spend two hours at breakfast. Read the paper. Talk on the phone."

Margo's June 24 send-off for her mom was touching. But things turned ugly fast. Within days, as if history was repeating itself, Margo publicly accused her cousin Jeanne Phillips, now author of the "Dear Abby" column, of a "crass" attempt to cash in on Eppie's legacy. In an exclusive story that I wrote for the *Tribune*, Margo said, "My mother has not been gone a full week yet, and I am highly offended by Jeanne Phillips's not-at-all-subtle move to make hay of my mother's death."

Margo was reacting to Jeanne's appearance on CNN's *Larry King Live* show, in which she tearfully expressed grief at her aunt's death. Margo said she also learned that Universal Press Syndicate, the distributor of "Dear Abby," was offering Jeanne's "farewell letter to Eppie," which she read on King's show, to all "Ann Landers" newspaper clients and other media, offering to let them run it free of charge, even if they didn't have the rights to "Dear Abby."

"This is not about grief," said Margo. "This is about new clients."

Unlike Margo, Jeanne Phillips realized that she wanted to be an advice columnist early on. She remembers first realizing that her mother was actually Dear Abby when Edward R. Murrow came to the family's home in 1958 to interview Popo for his *Person to Person* TV show. "At first the scrutiny was embarrassing. I was at an age when one doesn't want to be the center of attention," Phillips told me during a 2001 interview.

That age was fourteen, and her mother asked for her help in answering the increasing number of letters from teenagers, noting that it would be a good way to earn her allowance. "How much did I get?" asked Jeanne. "Maybe it was twenty-five cents."

During high school and into college at the University of Colorado, where she studied anthropology, Jeanne helped her mother with the column. She later cowrote more than half the shows that aired during the twelve years that "Dear Abby" expanded beyond print to become a syndicated radio show on CBS. (Eppie, too, had a radio show, in the early 1970s on NBC.) Jeanne cut back on column work for a few years after

206 • Rick Kogan

marrying a Los Angeles attorney but came back to the advice fold after her divorce, becoming the column's executive editor in 1980. "Mother said she needed me."

Jeanne had become the "Dear Abby" coauthor in 1987, though that was news to almost everyone when it was announced in December 2000. The announcement came in the form of a note from Popo that accompanied the first column that featured a photo of Popo and Jeanne: "With her talent, compassion and kind heart—and the common sense I like to say she inherited from her father and me—Jeanne has walked, not in my footsteps, but side by side with me.... I feel it's time she receives the recognition she deserves as my co-creator."

It was that announcement, coupled with Margo's entrée into the advice business, that inspired a *Tribune Magazine* cover story that I wrote about Eppie, Popo, and their daughters' work. While Margo and Eppie were forthcoming about their work and their feelings when being interviewed for the story, the "Dear Abby" team was tight-lipped. Popo did not give interviews, and Jeanne did so rarely. Finally she submitted to a phone interview, saying she and her mother worked eight hours each day, aided by a staff of six who sorted through the thousands of letters the column received each week. Beyond that, Jeanne said, "I'm not about to tell you our work habits. Let's just say I don't punch a clock." She did say that she did not read "Dear Prudence."

Jeanne's appearance on King's show the week after Eppie's death initiated a feud with Margo that mirrored the bitter and much-publicized battles between their mothers that added drama to the long-running competition of their advice columns.

A statement issued from Universal Press Syndicate in response to Margo's charges read: "Jeanne Phillips turned down interviews on several national television shows to discuss her aunt's death, including the 'Today' show. However, she felt obliged to fulfill the commitment she made [to appear on 'Larry King Live' this week]. . . . As a guest on the show, she could not control content or questions, but she answered the questions that were asked of her about her aunt with the utmost respect and sincerity. We regret that Ms. Landers' daughter and other 'Dear Abby' competitors see her efforts any other way."

Margo countered in the *Tribune*: "Though I was not asked, I, as her daughter, would not go on 'Larry King.' She's [Phillips's] had no relationship with my mother in decades. She has added to my distress at a very sad time in my life. Her [Phillips's] television appearance, flogging her 'grief' at my mother's death, in addition to her 'farewell' column, is beneath contempt, and as I understand it, is being seen for what it is: an excuse to flog her column. Such publicity grabs are just this side of disgraceful. I have been very protective of HER mother—and I am shocked that she would try to advance her career on the reputation of mine."

Jeanne had been scheduled to appear on King's show specifically to talk about the letter from a pedophile that she turned over to authorities. Understandably, the first portion of the program was devoted to the death of her aunt, during which she read her farewell, a portion of which said, "Aunt Eppie, I love you. I know it's time to say good-bye. But the words are impossible to say, because you will always live in my heart and in the hearts of the rest of your extended family. God bless you and keep you forever. Your loving niece."

On the King show, Jeanne said that when her mother was told of Eppie's death "She went to bed. . . . She did not take it well."

In the wake of the Margo and Jeanne battle, many people found it troubling that there had been no direct word from Popo; no call to Margo, no statement to the press. For all of the fussing and feuding the two had engaged in during their lives, the last few years, Eppie had told me, were filled with phone conversations and faxes back and forth. Others, most of them friends of Eppie's, were troubled that there was not going to be a funeral or memorial service, but that, Margo said, was the way Eppie wanted it. And so in the early evening of a Saturday late in August, Margo asked Marcy Sugar and Kathy Mitchell, and a handful of other relatives and employees, as well as a few of her friends, to join her at the eastern edge of Oak Street Beach for a subdued memorial and a scattering of Eppie's ashes on the lake, followed by a private dinner.

There would, however, be a public homage, when the Chicago City Council passed a two-page resolution to honor Eppie for epitomizing "Chicago with her strong opinion, her sage advice, her impeccable manners and quick wit" and announcing that a street sign—Ann "Eppie" Landers Way—would be installed at the corner of North Michigan Avenue from East Illinois Street to East North Water Street, in front of the Tribune Tower.

A letter accompanied the resolution. In it, the twins were linked (or confused) again. One sentence read: "It would be greatly appreciated if you forwarded this resolution to the family of 'Dear Abby.' "

When the weekend finally came, I sat down and read the final "Ann Landers" columns. It was a typically engaging mix of letters, some serious and some less so, and I would have written that on the Post-it notes but there was nobody to read them. I tried to find typographical errors, but there wasn't one. So all I could do was sit there and read the final day's column over and over, trying to determine whether it was epitaph or benediction, or maybe both.

The final letter to appear in the column read as follows: "Dear Ann Landers: I loved your column about how children misinterpret prayers. It reminded me of my own two little boys. Years ago, I heard them practicing, 'Mea culpa, mea culpa, mea maxima culpa'—except their version was, 'Me a Cowboy, Me a Cowboy, Me a Cowboy'—Betty in Wisconsin."

Eppie's response—"How adorable! I love it. Thanks for writing."—moved me to tears because it was accompanied by the realization that it was the final sentence in what had been more than forty-six years and an incalculable number of sentences. The readers were so important and essential to Eppie. On the twenty-fifth anniversary of the column in October 1980, she thanked her readers "for stretching my mind in a thousand different directions." The column so often spoke louder than the words that were in it. The seemingly innocuous gained resonance. The seemingly sappy became inspirational. An address or phone number was transformed into a life raft. That last sentence seemed to be screaming at me.

Now, a lot is made of final last words, from actress Tallulah Bankhead's "Codeine . . . bourbon" to actor/writer Noel Coward's "Goodnight my darlings, I'll see you tomorrow"; from scientist Charles Darwin's "I am not the least afraid to die" to James Thurber's "God bless . . . God damn."

Rereading that last "Ann Landers" column, that final sentence, I remembered the jaunty simplicity of the headline of the *Chicago Daily News* when it died on March 4, 1978, after 104 years: "So long, Chicago."

And so, Eppie's last words: "Thanks for writing."

Yes, I thought, those would do.

· LOT 1255C ·

Four Panels Listing Newspaper Featuring
"Ann Landers" Column Together with Photo
of Ann Landers Viewing These Panels

Dear Ann Landers. Dear Ann Landers. Dear Ann Landers. Dear Ann Landers.

The letters continued to pour in days, weeks, even months after Eppie died.

"Dear Ann Landers: I know you died but I was wondering if you might be able to answer one last question for me . . ." began one letter that arrived at the *Tribune* offices in late 2002. "Kind of spooky," said Kathy Mitchell. "And that's just one of a number we've seen. I guess some people think that Eppie is always going to be around, always able to help them, even after she's dead. What do you think she would think of what we're doing?"

"I think she'd be really proud," I said.

What she is doing, along with Marcy Sugar, is writing "Annie's Mailbox." It is an advice column that now runs in some seven hundred newspapers seven days a week. It was the brainchild of Rick Newcombe, president of the Creators Syndicate. "As you know better than anyone, we weren't sure this is what we should do," said Kathy. "Basically, it was, 'Hey, if we don't give it a shot we might be kicking ourselves in five years.' "

On July 28, 2002, the day after the final "Ann Landers" column appeared in the twelve hundred papers that carried it, "Annie's Mailbox" started to appear, usually in the space previously occupied by "Ann Landers." It was offered on its own or in many different configurations with a print version of Margo's "Dear Prudence" and a "Best of Ann Landers," which features exchanges previously published.

Trumpeting the debut of this trio, Newcombe said, "A sad event like Eppie's death will compel dozens if not hundreds of people to bring themselves to editors' attention in the hope that they will be selected to fill Eppie's shoes. Of course, we think we have the best package. One of Eppie's wishes was that there would be no 'Ann Landers' after she died, and we have respected that. But she certainly did not think that all advice columns should end with her passing."

The day after Eppie's death was made public, editors across the country began receiving a torrent of résumés, e-mails, and proposals from those already working in the advice business (in newspapers and on the Internet) and others who sensed the opportunity for a high-profile, high-paying job. "I don't see anyone dominating the genre like ['Ann Landers' and 'Dear Abby'] did for a long time, if ever," said Stephen Tibble, marketing director for Tribune Media Services, an international newspaper syndicate. "It takes time for a columnist to get established. It's not the sort of thing where you're going to have one person of their stature jumping in."

Eppie and Popo had been such dominant forces in the newspaper business (and such powerful cash cows for newspaper syndicates) that as early as 1985 people expressed worry about how they could ever be replaced. A front-page story by Steve Weiner in the *Wall Street Journal* pondered what might happen if the twin advice columnists ever retired. He wrote: "Neither of the 67-year-old sisters plans to retire. But that is scant comfort to some people who run newspapers. The advice field is thick with specialists in fields of advice as diverse as self-defense, senior citizens and sexual surrogates. But it is thin in sensible, general advisers. Editors wonder who will emerge to advise America."

A competing advice columnist of the time, Margaret Whitcomb, who wrote the column "Dear Meg," told the *Journal,* "They are a hard act to follow. I've had editors tell me they want a new voice. But I think those two will live to be 110." Eppie responded by saying, "I have no plans to retire. I intend to crank out this column as long as [readers] find me useful and the good Lord gives me the strength to do it."

After Eppie's death, some editors boldly declared they had already decided which syndicated advice columns would fill the space after the final "Ann Landers" column appeared. "I'm surprised that editors are already making decisions," said Brent Bierman, lifestyle editor of the Knight Ridder/Tribune News Service. "They feel they need to make decisions." He said there were about a half-dozen possible successors currently writing, but added, "we still don't know if a celebrity will sweep into the marketplace." He suggested one who might succeed if she wanted it was Oprah Winfrey.

Jeff Zaslow, who had been one of the two columnists who took Eppie's place when she left the *Sun-Times* for the *Tribune* in 1987, agreed with that assessment. He had left the advice business to return to the *Wall Street Journal* in 2001. (The other, Diane Crowley, daughter of the original Ann Landers, left the advice business in 1993.) Zaslow said, "[Oprah's] got the stature, and America already knows and trusts her. But that doesn't mean she's interested, or that she would be a good advice columnist. In some ways, hugging people with words is harder than hugging them on TV."

Or hugging them from bookshelves or radios or computers. The world often seems so awash in advice that it is little wonder that in the wake of Eppie's death, many people, most of them newspaper editors, questioned whether advice columns could remain viable or even necessary newspaper elements. Look at all the alternatives, they would tell you: online sites, radio call-in shows, TV gabfests, bookshelves that groan under the weight of the self-help publishing machine, encounter groups, self-empowerment seminars, and every sort of (Addictive Behavior) Anonymous organization.

In many ways Eppie and Popo can be credited for the American self-help craze. They not only helped reenergize and redefine a tired genre, but they unwittingly helped create the bulging bookshelves, the public confessions, and the problem parades that fill the nation's airwaves, and the dozens of people writing increasingly narrowly focused advice columns for newspapers and magazines and the Internet. Eppie succintly addressed why she believed people wrote to her in her 1975 book *Ann Landers Speaks Out:* "The mail represents every conceivable segment of society, every economic, social, and intellectual level. . . . Why do they write to Ann Landers? At first, it was mind-boggling. But now I understand it. They write to me for a variety of reasons. Some of my pen pals are ashamed to go to anyone they know. . . . Others write because a letter to Ann Landers costs only the price of postage. It's a cheap and easy way to get 'another opinion.' A visit to a counselor means an appointment, and bus fare. Then of course, there may be a fee."

When I asked Jeanne Phillips a few years ago, "Why do people write to advice columnists?" she said, "There's a crying need for it. My mail indicates that this country needs people who are willing to sit down and give straight-from-the-shoulder advice. . . . A lot of people don't have the money [for doctors or other professionals]. A lot of them are embarrassed about having a problem. They think it's a sign of weakness. They don't want their families to know."

I never did get to ask Popo, and, regrettably, Eppie's identical twin and lifelong rival will likely never be able to discuss the advice business. In early August 2002, in the form of an announcement that came as news to all readers and most editors, Jeanne told the press that her mother was suffering from Alzheimer's disease. The revelation came in response to an increasing number of media inquiries, most prompted by the questions that arose when there was no direct statement from Popo in the days after Eppie's death.

"Out of respect for my father and his wishes, I have not been at liberty to discuss my mother's Alzheimer's publicly," said Jeanne. "That may change one day, but right now, I hope it's enough for the people who love her to know that she's physically healthy and is receiving the best professional care in the world, surrounded by family who love her." She also said that the deterioration of her mother's memory had been slow, and that she had not been involved in the day-to-day business of the column for a couple of years.

The *Tribune,* which continued to carry "Dear Abby," decided not to publish "Annie's Mailbox," though it did begin to offer it on its online edition, along with Margo's "Dear Prudence" column, which also ran in print on Tuesdays in the "Tempo" section, and on Sundays in a new feature section called "Q."

At the time of Eppie's death, *Tribune* editor Ann Marie Lipinski told me, "Eppie is not replaceable. Our readers have made that clear. The question for news organizations isn't, 'Who's the next Ann Landers?' but 'What's the next act?' "

Some would point to Carolyn Hax, whose "Tell Me About It: Advice for the Under-30 Crowd" is put out by the *Washington Post;* the *New York Times* syndicate's Jane Rinzler Buckingham; Tara Solomon's "Advice Diva" for the *Miami Herald;* and Amy Alkon's syndicated "Advice Goddess." What these and other members of the new generation of advice columnists are doing is running chatrooms in black-and-white, forums for people to share not only their problems but to exchange solutions and personal experiences. The columns also function as sources of information about organizations that are in the business of providing help. But with real chatrooms, in addition to all the other advice avenues, now available, won't the flow of letters to newspaper advice columnists eventually slow to a trickle?

"Not if we are any indication," says Kathy Mitchell of "Annie's Mailbox." "The volume of mail has actually been increasing. We are getting about eight hundred e-mails every day."

"The most important aspect of newspaper advice columns is that they are able to disseminate information to millions of readers at once," says Marcy Sugar, Mitchell's coauthor. "There is a tremendous demand for advice, and most people want to get it from a nonjudgmental third party, especially if they consider that person to be a friend they can trust."

Most people in the business believe that the newspaper advice-giving game will continue to fragment, with specialty columns focused on such specific problem areas as teens, finance, sex, money, under thirty/over sixty, cars, cats—almost anything and everything.

More than a year after Eppie's death, the *Tribune* created a new general advice column called "Ask Amy." Its author, forty-three-year-old Amy Dickinson, was a veteran journalist, radio commentator, former lounge singer, and divorced mother with a fourteen-year-old daughter.

"Eppie's passing was a painful loss for readers," said Lipinski. "Her death created a void and we spent a great deal of time talking with readers about how to, or even if to, fill that void. It didn't take long to realize that this was something that readers wanted from the *Tribune* and we were determined to deliver it with a new and distinctive voice."

I was assigned to write the story that would announce to Chicago and the rest of the country the column's July 20 debut and tell people about Amy. For the interview I took her to Lincoln Park Zoo's Farm in the Zoo. She had grown up on a dairy farm in upstate New York and I wanted to see her feed hay to some cows. She thought that was a fun idea. So we wandered around the zoo, fed hay to some cows, and talked. Much of the conversation was about her move from Washington, D.C., to Chicago, her impressions of the city so far, other advice columnists, the fact that Margo's "Dear Prudence" column would no longer be running in the *Tribune,* and the demands of writing a seven-days-a-week column.

There was also, understandably, a lot of talk about Eppie.

"Reading her column when I was younger allowed me to listen to the national dialogue," Dickinson said. "People in Dallas, Iowa City, Savannah, Boston, Portland, and upstate New York were worried about the Vietnam War and alcoholism and, oh, yes, meddling mothers-in-law. Sometimes her column was just really entertaining, but reading that there are strangers out there who shared problems and concerns, that was a tremendous value. Ann Landers was a person of her time, and I'm a person very much of my time."

She said she was excited but "the other night I had a dream about being buried under envelopes. And I worry about trying to fill Eppie Lederer's pumps. She was really skilled at taking the national pulse, and her column over the years reflected the hopes, dreams, fears, and concerns of the great wide majority of the American public."

Eppie understood the role she played in popularizing advice and, in a sense, giving birth to the ever-growing market of advice/self-help/empowerment products that seem to have enveloped America. But she certainly would not have considered this "industry" to be her legacy, the vestiges of herself that she would leave behind for future generations.

Part of her true legacy could be found on March 4, 2003, when the Multiple Myeloma Research Foundation held a benefit dinner to raise funds to research this relatively unknown blood cancer. Eppie would have been moved by the story behind the inception of the MMRF, to learn that it was started by two women, Kathy Giusti and Karen Andrews. They are twins, and when Kathy was diagnosed with multiple myeloma in 1998, she and Karen created the MMRF. In five years, with little more than good intentions and boundless energy, the sisters have raised more than 17 million dollars.

On the night of the benefit dinner, Chicago was hit by a severe storm. Snow is something Chicagoans expect as late as March, and so the storm was no surprise. What was was that more than 700 people braved the weather and slippery streets to get to the Four Seasons Hotel. The MMRF benefit served as the launching pad for the Ann Landers Research Fund, established through a collaboration between Eppie's family, the MMRF, and the *Chicago Tribune.* And a check for $200,000 was presented to Northwestern University professor Dr. Seema Singhal, who directs the university's myeloma research.

There were a number of speeches, for example, from host

Dan Jansen, a former Olympic speed skater who had lost a sister to leukemia, and from sportscaster Bob Costas, who was presented the MMRF's public awareness award. There was also a screening of a short film. It featured Eppie. There were images of her in Vietnam, with Jules, in conversation, smiling, and laughing. As always, she looked great.

As the event ended, people began retrieving their coats, tying scarves tightly around their necks, and pulling hats snugly on their heads. By now the snow was whipping furiously outside, falling almost sideways due to the wind. My wife and I were out in the storm, trying desperately to find a cab when I realized that I had forgotten to take one of the evening's program books. So I rushed back into the hotel, into the empty ballroom, and grabbed one from a table.

I was putting it into my briefcase when I noticed its back cover. There was Eppie, in a beautiful photo that I remembered had appeared in the *Tribune Magazine* story I wrote about her in 2001. She was smiling. And across the bottom of the photo, in stylish script, were three simple words: "Still helping people."

Epilogue

Dear Eppie:

I'm sure you'll want to know, the auction was a lot stranger than I imagined. I did meet some very likable people. Almost all of them had been to a Bunte auction before. Indeed, for many of them, auctions seem to be a principal form of entertainment. They go to an auction somewhere in the Chicago area almost every weekend.

"It doesn't cost anything, unless you buy something," one woman told me. "And you can sometimes find some very good bargains."

I must have looked like a newcomer to this subculture— what was the tip-off?—because a man came up and said, "Here, I'll show you how to get a number." Though I didn't know what he was talking about and even said, "That's okay. I'm okay," a few minutes later I had a small cardboard card with the number 364 on it that would, when the auction started, allow me to bid on any of the bits and pieces of your life I wanted to own.

People were all over the place looking at your things, and I have to admit that some of them were new to me, no matter how many times I had spent just wandering around your apartment. I think I recognized some of the clothes that were hanging on a rack near the front door. They were all size 6. A few of the suits had expensive labels—Escada and Christian Dior—and there was one bizarre shawl, all psychedelic colors, like something from a production of *Hair*. I couldn't imagine you wearing that, but you must have. I did check the pocket of a stylish black jacket but I didn't find the dollar bill from our "cocaine night." I felt relieved.

Whenever we went out, you were dressed up, not just the way people used to dress up to go out to dinner but the way they would dress if they were going to dinner at the White House, which you did many times. Margo told me, when you were eighty-two, a little more than a year before you died, "She can still get into these St. John suits, and she'll say to me, 'I'm wearing a Bill Blass suit from thirty years ago,' and I'll say, 'You wretch.' Isn't she just the last of the red-hot mamas?"

Yes you were.

Life was very good to you, if your life can be judged by the things you owned and what those things say about you now that you're dead. Most of them were in Elgin, or at Butterfield's in San Francisco. Many of the really good items went to Butterfield's. It's a larger, more prestigious auction house, with clients spread around the globe. I sent for one of the Butterfield's catalogs and found that you were part of a special sale, actually the star of the sale. Here's the billing: "The Connoisseur's Sale: Including the Property of the Estate of Esther Lederer (Ann Landers)." Pictures and descriptions of your possessions filled the last 32 pages of the 229-page book.

There were 126 lots up for auction in San Francisco. Some were individual items, such as lot 2666, an "Italian Neoclassical Parcel Gilt Walnut Settee." I wouldn't have known what that was if there wasn't a picture of it in the catalog showing a stylish bench. I remember that bench but I can't remember if I ever sat on it. Lot number 2717 was a collection of photos of you with celebrities and politicians. Whoever bought that got pictures of you with Ronald and Nancy Reagan, Bill Clinton, Bill Cosby, and others, presumably not celebrated enough to list by name.

Some people were confused—even angry—that so many of your things, some seeming to be so personal, were put up for auction. Indeed, auction items did include such things as personal scrapbooks you created to memorialize your career, your high school and college yearbooks, and honorary degrees you received. One person at the auction in San Francisco, looking at some of your clothes awkwardly hung on male mannequins, asked "Who's doing this to her? This is like a suburban garage sale."

In an interview with the Associated Press, Margo explained her decision to auction your possessions: "Because of who she was I thought that people who wanted to have that kind of connection to her should have that chance."

A few people in Elgin seized the opportunity for such a connection, though none I talked to was the kind of person I had initially come looking for. Though many told me they admired you and read you every day, none could share a specific story about how the column had changed their lives.

I did get a letter a few days later from a man named Edward A. Karns, Ph.D., from Homer Glen, Illinois. He wrote to say that talking to me at the auction reminded him "of an experience I had early in the sixties when I served as an elementary principal in the Columbus, Ohio area. At the time a vast majority of elementary school principals were single women who had devoted their lives to the education of children.

"Ms. Landers was the keynote speaker at the Ohio Elementary Principals' Association conference, which I attended. She began her presentation by stating that she had struggled with her topic for the evening. Her first consideration was elementary school principals. Secondly, she considered speaking about problems since so many of her clients wrote to her for advice about problems. Her third consideration was to speak about sex. She stated that she had decided to combine all three topics and speak about the sex problems of elementary school principals. Forty years later I still chuckle about her clever introduction."

Dr. Karns and his wife, Judith, deal in antiques. It's not their profession but their hobby. They successfully bid on about a dozen auction items, including some books, bronze medallions presented to you as awards, a sweater, and a watercolor. They sold a few things to other dealers, but they gave an autographed copy of one of Margaret Truman's books to their son, who collects political memorabilia, and have decided to keep the sweater forever. "It's black sweater with jewels all over it," Karns told me. "It's . . . what's the word for it? Gaudy, that's it. But it was hers and we like having it."

Another person, Jorie Maciejewski, an account manager for a life insurance company, wrote me an e-mail: "I met Ann in 1998 at a benefit for [the abolition of] land mines. At the time I had just started a new relationship with a man that I worked with and, as in all brand new relationships, was still in the getting comfortable/getting to know you stage. Also, we had to hide our dating from others in the office to prevent any gossip that might also cause stress to our blooming romance. At the benefit, Ann happened to be walking past me at the time and stopped to chat with a few people. I stopped to introduce myself and give her praise for her column. And before I knew it, I had asked her, 'What are your thoughts on office romances?' Ann replied, 'They're great if you can find them.' Well, I found mine and held on tight. And now I've been happily married for over one year. So, that's my story. It's short but sweet but I love to tell it."

Mrs. Maciejewski bought a box of books written by you for $25.

Another woman, social worker Sandy Bratthauer, bought a bureau, a brass headboard, and a love seat for less than $100. She said that she wasn't going to fix any of the items' flaws, the nicks and scratches. "I want Ann Landers in my house," she said.

Many of the things being auctioned were flawed. A lot of it was, really, sort of junky, and most auction houses don't accept or try to sell such bruised and battered items. But this was different. One of the brothers who run the Elgin auction house said so. "These things were chipped by her," Kevin Bunte told me. "We wouldn't even take that desk if it wasn't hers. Many columns were written there and tens of thousands of letters passed over it."

The desk was a real mess, the sort of thing one finds

propped up against a wall in an alley; beaten and worn and a pain in the ass for garbage men to haul away. But on Sunday, one young man saw beauty in the battered desk and bought it. His name is Dan Savage. He lives in Seattle now but is Chicago born and raised.

For nearly twelve years, Savage has written "Savage Love," a syndicated weekly column that specializes in extremely explicit advice about the kinds of sexual activities acts that cannot be mentioned in a "family newspaper." It runs in seventy U.S. newspapers, such as the *Village Voice* and the *Onion*. It also appears in papers in China, Israel, and Europe. You would have liked him, and he would have been thrilled to meet you, though you certainly would have been shocked by the sorts of letters he gets.

You'd probably have been shocked, too, to learn that I bought something Saturday. I don't know quite what came over me, but I got caught up in the auction fever and before I knew it I was raising my little 364 sign and was the new owner of lot 221: "Four Brass Owl Figures, including bookends." My winning bid was $45. With tax and what's called the buyer's premium, the total cost came to $49.34.

It didn't take me long to get over my auction anxiety. In fact, I started to think that I was shopping. I was tempted to buy so many things of yours, even copies of books I already had. As I was poking around some pictures before they went up for auction, I started thinking that what I really would like to find would be a picture of you standing with Johnny Carson. Wouldn't that be the perfect definition of a certain American time? You, the person everybody woke up to, America's mom, fixing breakfast and otherwise getting us ready to face the day, and Johnny, sort of like America's dad, tucking us in every night with enough good humor to convince us that the world would still be spinning when we got up.

I found no such picture and before leaving I put in a bid on some items to be auctioned on Sunday: a couple of cocktail glasses on which owls were etched; a package of photos, nothing very notable; and an item I really wanted, your senior Central High School yearbook, class of 1936.

I couldn't be in Elgin on Sunday because I had to attend a memorial service for another newspaper legend. You knew Tom Fitzpatrick. He was a Chicago newspaper character that we both admired. We, and everybody else, called him Fitz.

While his memorial service was taking place, the rest of your things were being sold, being scattered to homes and other places. The sale in San Francisco netted about $250,000. Someone paid $29,125 for a rare and important print, "Enchanted Owl," by Kenojuak Ashevak, signed, dated, and annotated by the artist. Someone paid $21,075 for a George III mahogany sideboard that had been prominently situated in your apartment foyer. Someone paid $8,812.50 for a pair of Napoleon III gilt and bronze seven-light candelabra, each depicting a winged Nike in flowing robes. Someone paid $7,050 for a George III mahogany grandfather clock, made in England in the eighteenth century.

Also sold was a batch of correspondence, documents, news clippings, photos, and other items. Butterfield's labeled these your "V.I.P. Files." They fetched $5,875 from the Chicago Historical Society. Included were ninety-five folio scrapbooks containing a complete run of clippings of your columns from 1955 to 2000; the manuscript for *Ann Landers Encyclopedia A to Z*; three hundred manuscripts for the NBC radio show *This Is Ann Landers*; approximately fifteen hundred pages of various speeches; and an electric typewriter.

"Adding these wonderful items from a Chicago icon shows our commitment to documenting the contemporary history of Chicago," said Lonnie Bunch, president of the CHS. "Eppie Lederer was a wonderful woman, a great person and a pillar in Chicago's social, cultural and media community. We are honored to have part of her legacy here."

The Elgin auction made $55,000. "We're happy," co-owner Kevin Bunte told me. "It's unusual to have two auctions, but there was much Butterfield's did not want. We have a relationship with that house and so offered to auction what they didn't take to San Francisco. The mood here, I thought, was very respectful. You never can tell what you're going to get at a celebrity auction. Some people want something for a pop culture joke. But Ann Landers fans came from all walks of life."

A Baccarat crystal frog went for $190; a black lacquer letter-holder holding some personalized Post-it notes netted $375; and a carved wooden owl fetched $1,600. Your 1992 Cadillac Brougham was bought by an Indiana car dealer for $9,000.

The auctions were over about the same time as the memorial service for Fitz. I wandered with the white-haired crowd over to Stefani's 437, a bar/restaurant that used to be known as Riccardo's and was a hangout for newspaper folks, where everybody would tell stories about Fitz and the good old newspaper days. I didn't stay long. Death, whether up close or in memorials, puts me in a solitary mood. I wanted some quiet, so I made my way over to the Billy Goat Tavern, another newspaper hang-out that was Mike Royko's favorite bar.

The walk was short but chilly. In Chicago, mid-November usually means two things: winter and Christmas are on the way; inside the bar, which was wonderfully empty, Tito the waiter was already stringing holiday decorations.

The walls of the Billy Goat are covered with the names and pictures of Chicago journalists, most of them dead and most of them forgotten. I ordered a drink, walked to a table, and sat down, feeling like I was surrounded by ghosts.

I reached in my briefcase for—yes, sorry—a pack of ciga-rettes and was surprised to touch something hard, metallic. I pulled it out and started to laugh. It was one of your owls. Now, I'm not much of a superstitious guy, but I decided to forgo the cigarette and fished around for the other three owls I'd bought the day before at the auction.

I put the owls, none taller than about four inches, on the table and stared at them for a long time, thinking about life— Fitz's, mine, Mike's, and yours.

Mike won the Pulitzer. So did Fitz, the last Pulitzer pre-sented for deadline reporting. He won it for a 1968 story about antiwar protesters who rampaged through Chicago one night. He ran with the mob and then ran back to the paper, where he banged out the story in twenty minutes.

You never won a Pulitzer Prize. How could you? The Pulitzer committee has never handed out an award for advice. But that never troubled you. "I would rather be on a hundred refrigerator doors than win the Pulitzer Prize," you said enough times to make me believe that of the many things you said, this was among the most important and personal.

How many refrigerator doors did your column appear on? What an astonishing number that must be. I thought about that for a while and soon—maybe because of the Christmas decorations going up and the whiskey going down—I was thinking about Jimmy Stewart. There he was, real as life in my mind, as George Bailey in Frank Capra's *It's a Wonderful Life*.

It's impossible to measure completely the impact that a person's life, however ordinary or extraordinary, has on the other people, the events, and the environment in which that life is led. Capra gave it a good shot, letting George Bailey see what his world would have been like if he had not lived in it: letting him see Bedford Falls as a harsh and dreadful place; the kindly pharmacist as a tortured town drunk; and his beautiful wife as an unhappy spinster.

It's a wonderful life. What a great title. It would certainly suit you: short, snappy, to the point. And I wondered if it would be possible to look at your life in the same fantastical fashion, what would you see? How many lives changed for the better by something read in your column? How many alcoholics discovered AA there? How many parents of gay kids learned to love and accept their children? How many kids will grow up into a world in which some forms of cancer have cures? Oh, hell, how many people stopped smoking and lived an extra fifteen years? How much better is this world for your having been in it?

Eventually, that Jimmy Stewart vision vanished. But, sitting there with four of your owls, that last question turned into its own answer: How much better is this world for your having been in it.

Wayne Loder

PUBLIC AWARENESS COORDINATION
FOR COMPASSIONATE FRIENDS

Michigan

Ours was the perfect American dream family. Married in 1976, my wife, Pat, and I were blessed with our beautiful daughter, Stephanie, and, three years later, our son, Stephen. With good jobs, a nice house, and plenty of time with the kids, our family and our lives seemed complete. In our spare time as a family, we'd explore the park, visit the school playground, and busy ourselves picking blueberries or raspberries. Our lives were so wonderful, so alive. The future was ours. Then it turned upside down.

On March 20, 1991, Pat was driving with our children seat belted beside her. Stephanie was eight and Stephen had just turned five. Making a left-hand turn onto our street, Pat's car was hit by a high-speed sport motorcycle. It struck on the passenger side front, spinning the car sideways. EMS and fire rescue units raced to the scene as Pat screamed for her children. A kindly passerby held her tightly in his arms to comfort and restrain her. Despite valiant efforts by paramedics and then by emergency room doctors at nearby Hudson Valley Hospital, Stephen could not be resuscitated. Stephanie was transported to the hospital and stabilized. The motorcyclist was killed, while Pat was hospitalized with minor injuries.

Stephanie was then transported by helicopter to University of Michigan Children's Hospital where tests confirmed everyone's fears: she had suffered brain death. After a quick conference on the phone, Pat and I agreed to donate Stephanie's organs, knowing that would have been her wish, that in dying she might save another child.

But life became for us absolute blackness. There was no purpose, or meaning—no reason to go on. Every day was a challenge for survival. Our energy was zapped by sleepless nights. We were on a constant emotional roller coaster and the tears flowed easily. A month after the accident, I returned to work. One day a customer, a person I knew as a friend, laid a piece of paper on the counter, smoothing it with his hands. It was an Ann Landers column in which a bereaved mother had written, seeking Ann's advice. She recommended that the woman contact The Compassionate Friends, a non-profit self-help bereavement organization for families following the death of a child. My friend had called that phone number and learned of a chapter about ten miles from where I worked.

A week later, Pat and I walked into the building where the meeting was to be held and couldn't believe the warm, friendly greeting we received. There were hugs instead of handshakes—and an opportunity to truly talk about what had happened. We were heartened by the fact that even as we told our stories, shed tears, and made friendships, we could see that others had survived—and if they could, so could we.

A year afterward, Pat and I decided we had been so helped by The Compassionate Friends, we wanted to give back by not just becoming involved with the organization, but by starting what was to be called the Lakes Area Chapter in Michigan near our home, a chapter that over the upcoming years helped hundred of bereaved families just like ours.

As Pat and I worked on a local level, we also became involved on the national level, taking over the editorship of two national newsletters. In September 2000 Pat was named executive director of The Compassionate Friends and I was asked to serve on TCF's Community Awareness Committee. Shortly thereafter I decided to sell the small retail store business I had founded and run for twenty-four years. When I mentioned the impending sale to the TCF board president, he offered me what would be a new position, Public Awareness Coordinator. Now I work to spread the word about an organization that helped me so much and was held in such high esteem by Ann Landers.

It is unlikely that anyone in the history of TCF gave the organization more of a public awareness boost than Ann Landers. Researching the organization for an article I wrote, I found one letter that Ann published from a reader who first made her aware of the organization and the help she had received in early 1978, the same year the organization was incorporated in the United States with forty "branches." Each time Ann would mention TCF in her column, which she did often, our organization would receive hundreds, if not thousands, of calls and communications.

Today, thanks to Ann and thousands of volunteers, there are nearly six hundred chapters serving all fifty states and thirty countries. In the United States, more than fifteen thousand people attend local chapter meetings each month. Outreach is provided to more than two hundred thousand bereaved families, as well as professionals, each month through chapter newsletters, phone calls, notes, and personal visits.

Ann Landers opened my eyes to an organization that I credit with saving my life. I only wish I could have met her in person to tell her what she meant to me and to tell her that today Pat and I have indeed survived, with the help of Compassionate Friends and our two wonderful subsequent children, Chris and Katie. The world does go on. It goes on without our Stephanie and Stephen. And it will go on without Ann Landers. But it will be a far, far better place because they lived in it.

Bill Kurtis and Donna LaPietra

TV PRODUCER-HOST
PRODUCER-PARTY PLANNER

Chicago

D ONNA: Neither of us were regular readers of Eppie's column but like many people we would occasionally get pulled in by a provocative headline. I had gotten to know her over the years. We met at social events. She often attended benefits I was chairing for such places as Steppenwolf Theatre or Lincoln Park Zoo. And we would meet at private parties. I got a special kick when she would attend the rather large Christmas parties that Bill and I had every year. One year, Oprah dropped in, another year, Michael Jordan. And Eppie was certainly a star of their magnitude. And she was a great guest. She was the life of a party. She was a great conversationalist. She danced up a storm. She was a great flirt, a slightly tamer version of Mae West.

But we really didn't know each other well. So I had no idea what to expect when I was invited for a one-on-one tea at her apartment a few years ago. I was certainly flattered to be

236 • Rick Kogan

asked, because she had always struck me as a "no-nonsense" sort of person, not one likely to waste her time unless she genuinely was interested in something or someone.

She greeted me at the door in a fabulous floor-length red brocade house gown that clasped at the waist. As we walked into the living room for tea, she said, "I just thought it was time we got to know each other better." She was really crazy about Bill and though she thought we were a great match—which was good since we'd been together for twenty years—I believe she wanted to be sure she had sized up Bill's young lady correctly. And if she had, she knew she might be in for a lively and interesting conversation.

As we talked, I realized how much I loved the way her voice jabbed at the air—coming from one side of her mouth, it had a hard edge to the sound of it, a little tough and of the streets. For someone who gave advice for a living—I discovered that day and throughout our friendship—she was a remarkably good listener. She really wanted to know, to see if there wasn't some tilt on things she hadn't tried out.

She told me that she was worried that I was overextending myself with too many charity groups, and perhaps neglecting personal needs and those closest to me.

I told her, though, that I had had the good fortune through these associations to meet so many wonderful people. "Donna," she said, "take it from me. You already know too many people. Cut back." Did I listen? No. Should I have? Most likely it was the best advice I'd ever been given.

BILL: Ann Landers asked *me* for advice!

She called me when she was approached about cooperating with the local producers of an episode of *Biography* about her life. She was worried that some of the personal aspects of her life—her divorce, the rivalry with her sister—might play out on TV in a negative fashion. I told her, "So much of this is already known. You have always allowed your readers to benefit from the insights that have grown from your own life. And truly, you have a life worthy of a biography. A life that has set you apart—you've seen the heights, you've talked to more people than most journalists ever dreamed of and, yes, you have also walked the journey of a personal life filled with the problems and tensions that make you no different from everyone else. So, there's no question, let it be shared."

I'm proud to say she took my advice and she did go along with the producers. She invited Donna and me to join her and a very small group of friends to watch the show. She seemed pleased and at a dinner following the show, she didn't just bask in compliments and praise. There she was, peppering the gathering with questions about current events and issues. She was always so curious, so eager to stay on top of things.

DONNA: We both miss her. Christmas won't be the same. But what a legacy she leaves. Her greatest gift was to the people who read her column. They learned that problems do have answers, not easy ones necessarily. She let people know that it was important to confront the problems, to know that conflicts need to be resolved. She pointed people toward the path to fulfillment and happiness.

William W. Greaves

CITY OF CHICAGO COMMISSION
ON HUMAN RELATIONS

Chicago

My first interaction with Ann Landers was in 1991. I was training for the Chicago Marathon, and my route took me down East Lake Shore Drive. One day I passed this short, well-dressed woman in spiked heels. I was wearing my orange running shorts with black polka dots and as I passed her all of a sudden I heard this wolf whistle and Ann Landers yelled, "Nice legs, sweetie."

That's the same year the Chicago Commission on Human Relations established the Chicago Gay and Lesbian Hall of Fame, which recognizes the volunteer and professional achievements of lesbians and gay men, their organizations, and their friends, as well as their contributions to the lesbian and gay community and to the City of Chicago. Induction into the Hall of Fame symbolizes that the recipient either made a contribution with far-reaching effects on the quality of life for Chicago's lesbian and gay community or the city of Chicago, or made a significant long-term contribution to the well-being of Chicago's lesbian and gay community. As the director/community liaison to the Advisory Council on Lesbian, Gay, Bisexual, and Transgender Issues, I'm involved in the nomination process.

I remember one letter to Ann Landers that was really a touchstone, because Ann changed her mind about the basis for homosexuality. It appeared in 1997 and was from a fifteen-year-old boy who was contemplating suicide because he had realized that he was gay. He was scared and confused.

Her response was excellent. She told him that he wasn't alone, that 10 percent of people on the planet were gay. Then she mentioned famous gay people like Alexander the Great, Leonardo DaVinci, Michelangelo, actor Rock Hudson, rock star Freddie Mercury, author Truman Capote, poet Allen Ginsberg, and playwright Tennessee Williams. She said, firmly and without equivocation, that homosexuals are born, not made, and advised him to seek counseling.

I always thought she was very levelheaded and supportive in her advice to most people. That letter in particular was very moving. And it says something that she chose to respond to it in print, that she found it that important. She made it an important issue.

Though she wasn't always supportive of the notion that homosexuality is a result of genetics, one of her great characteristics was that she learned. To watch her change her opinion was interesting. When she did she provided a voice for people who weren't in the mainstream, who lived in rural areas or small towns. She was one of the few public figures who supported gays and lesbians. She gave affirmation to people who otherwise wouldn't have gotten it.

When people are nominated for the Gay and Lesbian Hall of Fame, there is a procedure that is generally followed. The nominations come through a community group or neighborhood organization. There are forms to be filled out. Someone writes up a nomination, provides documentation of the person's achievements or contributions, and then a committee of previous inductees meets and chooses from those nominated.

But that's not how Ann Landers was nominated. At the time of her death there was a display of previous inductees in the window of a video store on Halsted Street. One morning her obituary from the *Tribune* was taped to the window. On it someone had written, simply and anonymously, "We respectfully nominate Ann Landers."

Although she has not been inducted yet, this may have been the most grassroots Hall of Fame nomination ever—in keeping with Ann's mass appeal.

Dr. B. Duncan McKinlay

PSYCHOLOGIST

Toronto, Canada

I would say that I knew I had some sort of secret since the age of seven. I had different impulses than other people have, like tics. I'd try to suppress them. If you think of what it's like to be covered with mosquito bites and not be able to scratch them, that's what it's like to try to suppress tics. I didn't understand what they were, I just knew I was probably going to get ostracized for doing them. So I'd try everything I could to keep them in.

I was good at hiding my tics. When I had a tic, I'd pretend like I was yawning and make yawning noises. Of course I'd get in trouble for that. Then I'd make noises and pretend like it was a song. I'd find ways of camouflaging.

By the time I got to high school, life was just something to be endured. I didn't have a sense of what was different about me. I just didn't feel good about myself. I felt strange. I wrote off many potential friends because I thought if they knew everything about me, about the tics, they wouldn't like me. I was still trying to suppress tics, which led to other problems. I was irritable, explosive, and socially obtuse because I was so preoccupied with fighting my symptoms. I didn't expect an answer at this point as to why I seemed to be somehow "wrong." I just had the grim acceptance that I was not going to fit in.

You never know the day you wake up that that's the day that will change your life forever. For me, it was in April 1992. I was eighteen, in my last year of high school getting ready to go off to university. I went home for lunch that day, I remember. I came home for lunch nearly every day and always did the same thing; I'd flip through the comics, read the "Ann Landers" column, eat, and go back to school. I remember I was running late that day so I almost decided not to read the column. I was eating my sandwich as I read it, and then my jaw dropped.

There, in the column, was a letter from a woman seeking to create awareness about Tourette's syndrome (TS), a neurological disorder that at the time was believed to affect roughly 1 million people in North America, including this woman's daughter. She described some of the common symptoms of TS—constant humming, throat clearing, clicking sounds—as well as other obsessive/compulsive behaviors and concentration issues. She asked that people have tolerance and compassion when they meet people who exhibit such tics and gestures.

I was short of breath. It was like an adrenaline shot. This voice in my head that had been telling me since age seven, "There's really something wrong with you, Duncan. You're a freak." This voice was now doing jumping jacks, saying, "That's me!" I read the column a number of times. Someone was describing me and there were other people like me! I remember she said that the tics weren't intentional. That people with TS can't help themselves. It was so validating of the internal struggle I'd been going through. That day, before the end of the day, I had told my mom and dad and three best friends that I thought I had TS.

It didn't make everything all right immediately, but it was the beginning of the end for a very depressed victim. I went to McMaster University in Hamilton, Ontario. It was a much bigger city and there were lots of doctors there. They passed me around from doctor to doctor, until I was ultimately given a diagnosis of TS in December 1992.

Now I'm a psychologist and a national director of the TS Foundation of Canada. I did my doctoral research on TS and am one of the leading psychologists working in the area of TS in Canada. Before I developed my own neuropsychological model of tic formation (called "The Incidental Associations" model, now taught in some undergraduate university courses), the research on what was happening in the brain in TS had reached an impasse. Researches knew the areas that were involved, but they hadn't been able to explain why tics appeared and looked the way they did.

My pie in the sky dream is to someday start a clinic that works with children and adolescents with TS, but also with disorders like rage/attention deficit hyperactivity disorder, obsessive compulsive disorder, and learning disabilities—all of which fall under the umbrella of Tourette's. My clinic would go under the name "Life's a Twitch!," the current name of my website and also my presentation/consultation business. This clinic would offer assessments, diagnoses, and treatment, as well as promote public awareness through school inservices, public presentations, articles, and books.

As soon as I found out Ann Landers had died, I wrote a eulogy on my website. In a sense, everything I do—the number of people I touch with my presentations, my writing, my website—is all because of Ann. I wrote something along the lines of, "Savior of millions and internationally known for her kindness and generosity, Ann Landers has passed away. For those of you who didn't know her: if you've been touched by me, you've been touched by Ann. If you'd like to know more about this phenomenal lady, click here. Rest well, ma'am."

Sharon Soderlund

DAUGHTER

Minneapolis

My mother, Myrtle Julia Cecelia Noyd Dunshee, was born on July 7, 1905. She was the fourth child of eight children born to Frank and Amanda Noyd, Swedish immigrants who farmed near Taylor's Falls, Minnesota. She met my dad, Ted Dunshee, at a St. Patrick's Day dance. They were married in 1936 and were together until my dad died in January 1987. That hit her hard. She became depressed and afraid of staying at home alone at night.

Her short-term memory was starting to fail, and she was unable to remember to take her medicines or to do much cooking. My Auntie Rose lived next door and watched over Mom and made her meals. One day Mom spent several hours at my aunt's house, and after having supper there, Mom remembered that she'd forgotten to take in her paper that day—or maybe it was her mail. It had snowed that day and was cold. Mom told Rose that she was going back to her house to get her mail, and Rose told her to just leave it. Rose went to the kitchen to do the dishes. Mom went out the front door of Auntie's house and headed toward her house. It wasn't until Rose finished the dishes that she discovered Mom was gone—and that she'd gone out without her winter coat.

In the meantime, Mom had fallen on the icy sidewalk on her way to her house, and she couldn't get up. We think she was on the sidewalk in the cold ten or fifteen minutes before a neighbor who was walking to the bus stop found her.

At that point for her own safety, we decided that Mom could no longer stay in her own house. She needed to live at the Augustana Home, a nursing home associated with her church. Mom had volunteered in the coffee shop at the home almost every Friday for most of her life, and she used to bake pies and cakes and take them to the home for the residents who would have coffee there. Mom knew the staff, and many residents were friends from church. She always said that was where she wanted to be if or when she could no longer stay in her own home.

Except for gout and arthritis, Mom was in relatively good health. She was resilient. She had triple bypass heart surgery a few years before, surgery for breast cancer, and some eye surgery for cataracts and glaucoma, but she was still getting around and was in good spirits. Mom suffered a massive stroke on June 2, 1990—the day that Russian president Mikhail Gorbachev came to Minneapolis. My daughter Karin was a member of Angelica Cantanti, a children's choir that sang for him at the airport that day, and she was interviewed on TV. I remember thinking how proud Mom would be if only she would have been able to see that.

The nursing home staff found her on the floor that morning; they called me and rushed Mom to the hospital. We met Mom in the emergency room. When the nurse asked, "Do you know who this is?" Mom answered, "Sharon." That was her last word.

They whisked her away for a CAT scan, and when she emerged from that test, she was completely unresponsive. The doctor told me I had to decide then and there if she should be put on a respirator, because her breathing was getting really ragged, and he said that she would die within a few minutes without life support. After questioning him for a few minutes, I learned that they would probably know in three days which way it would go. By then, either she'd be a lot better or a lot worse. They'd repeat the CAT scan on day three to determine the full extent of the stroke and I could take her off the respirator then, if it was apparent that she was dying. I wanted to give Mom every chance to recover, so we put her on life support.

That second CAT scan showed extensive brain damage, and I decided that she would not want to be kept alive with extraordinary means, so we took her off the respirator and later removed the IV. That was no an easy decision. We are a pro-life family and I agonized over what I was doing. I had a vague memory that when I was about twelve, Mom told me that she never wanted to be kept alive by machines. I don't remember having talked with her about her end-of-life wishes later in life, so I wasn't sure what her wishes were when she suffered the stroke. I didn't know if I had done the right thing, but I asked the nurses to keep putting ice chips in her mouth every two hours.

Mom's Bible was in the room. She had always kept it at home, on the same spot on the dining room bureau. She kept important things inside—and also any cash my parents had on hand. She said if anyone ever broke into their house, they'd never think to look in the Bible!

The day after the IV was disconnected, my cousin Dan Strum was visiting my mom, who was in a deep coma. He started reading that Bible and found something in it. He called me immediately because what he found was an "Ann Landers" column from April 4, 1971, that appeared in the *Minneapolis Tribune*. He started to read it to me.

"Dear Ann Landers: The letter from the children of the 90-year-old woman who fell out of bed at the nursing home and broke her hip prompted me to write a letter on instruction to my sons. I am sending you a copy in the hope that you will print it. Perhaps it will encourage some of your readers to write similar letters to their children. My thanks and God bless—Sane, Sensible and Realistic.

Dear Sons: This letter is not a request, it is an order. I have tried to live with dignity and I want to die the same way. If my fate is such that I should become old and ill and unable to make a rational decision, you are herby instructed to give my attending physician orders that he must not attempt to prolong my life by using extraordinary measures. If I am stricken with an illness which is irreversible, and unable to speak for myself, please speak for me. I want no surgery, no cobalt, no blood transfusions and no intravenous feedings. Instead, please see to it that the physician gives me plenty of medication and sedatives. This letter of instruction will relieve you of the burden of making the decision. It is made. My thanks and my love, Mother."

Dan stopped reading for a second and then he said, "There's more."

It was a note written in my mother's hand on the column, meant for my husband, Joe (a physician), and me: "Dear Sharon & Joe, Please note, this is my sincere wish too. Your mother, Sharon. Myrtle (Mrs. Theo. Dunshee) 1980." I burst into tears.

I really believe that the Holy Spirit was in Mom's room at the Augustana Home as she lay there unable to make her wishes known—and that Dan received divine guidance to walk across the room to her desk and open her Bible that night. I believe that it was a sign from God and Ann Landers—AND my mother!—that I had made the right decision. She died ten days later. She is buried in the cemetery outside Taylor's Falls, not far from the town of Shafer, where she was born and where she grew up.

Mike Leep

OWNER OF CAR DEALERSHIPS

South Bend, Indiana

Fate is an amazing thing. I was going out of town for a week, to the West Indies with my family, and I passed through Chicago and picked up the newspaper and saw that Ann Landers's limo was going to be auctioned. There was no way I would have heard about that if I hadn't picked up that paper, but I thought I had to have this woman's car. I didn't want it as a souvenir. I wanted to put it to good use.

I bought it sight unseen. I wasn't in town. I had a friend go up to the auction house in Elgin and buy it. I got it for $9,000. I was willing to go to $20,000. I wanted it because I truly grew up reading Ann Landers. I started reading her column when I was fifteen. I'm fifty-five now. That's a long time. What I liked about her was that she wasn't afraid to say, "Hey I'm wrong. I made a mistake." That's extremely important for anyone giving advice. And she did it in front of millions of people. She also had insight into what makes the world go round. Did I get any advice from her? I'm an old school guy. I lock it all inside. But she did so much for so many people. When she died I was sad. It was the end of an era.

I have a feel for cars and I thought, "Her limo, man. Now that's something." I also felt connected to her in that she and Father Hesburgh (Rev. Theodore M. Hesburgh, president emeritus of the University of Notre Dame) were good friends. I knew he'd been in the car and other wonderful people had been in the car. There was no other reason why I bought it except that it was Ann Landers's car.

I had it completely restored. Don't get me wrong. It was in good condition. But it had fifty-eight thousand miles on it. It needed new tires, some small mechanical stuff done to it. So I had my guys fix it up. Now it's like the day it came out of the factory. It's a 1992 Cadillac, twenty-two-foot stretch limo. No, there's no bar in it. But there's a glass partition, a phone, and a stereo. I also got, along with all the ownership papers for the car, a copy of her death certificate. I had to pay an extra $125 for the chauffeur's hat and her license plate—AL 55— but I had to have them.

In all I put about another $4,000 into the car to bring it up to pristine condition. I cleaned it and put it away. My plans for the car? We do a lot in the South Bend community. I'm thinking of auctioning off a night in the limo, for prom nights and different events, and then whatever money is raised will be given to charity. That's my plan. I know Ann Landers always stepped to the plate to help different organizations. She was not a taker. She gave a lot. Sure I'll take a ride in the car, but I'll be the guy in the chauffeur's seat.

Dan Savage

SYNDICATED ADVICE COLUMNIST

Seattle

W here was I when I heard that Ann Landers had died? I was afraid someone would ask me that. Intending no disrespect, I share the following information only because it's God's own truth: I was sitting on the toilet reading David Brock's *Blinded by the Right* and listening to the radio. It's fitting that I was—I'm avoiding the obvious rhyme out of respect—crapping when I heard the news. You see, for years, I've been getting letters from people who wanted me to shit all over Ann Landers. It seems that a lot of people who read my column didn't like Ann or her twin sister, Abigail Van Buren, much, and those people would write me and ask me to rip into them. Here's a letter from the fall of 2000: "Why do you spend so much time bashing Ralph Nader? Why don't you stick to your field and bash Ann Landers, that conservative, tight-assed, reactionary bitch?"

Some people may not know that I dedicated my first

book, a collection of "Savage Love" columns, to Ann Landers (as well as Abigail Van Buren and Xaviera Hollander). Landers invented the modern advice column, and while we third-generation advice columnists may use language she wouldn't approve of, all of our columns are modeled after hers. The conversational tone, the guest experts, debates with readers who disagree with you—that's Ann Landers.

While Landers never could wrap her bouffant around the fact that most cross-dressers are straight men, she was more progressive than some of my readers were willing to give her credit for. She didn't pressure women to stay in bad marriages, her position on homosexuality changed with the times, and she was pro–gun control. Two years ago, Landers came out in favor of legalizing prostitution! Her column ran in twelve hundred papers, and in some of those papers, her voice was the only progressive voice her readers ever heard. Landers may not have entertained questions about shooting beer up your butt or fucking your sister, but she didn't have to. She made it possible for a freak like me to answer those questions.

A few months after her death I was put on cloud nine by something I bought: I got . . . I got . . . a desk! A used desk! A really old, beat-up desk! It's covered with ink stains and pieces of Scotch tape, the veneer is peeling, and it's even missing a drawer. It's not so much the used desk itself that I'm giddy about, but the person who used it: Ann Landers. Items from the estate of Eppie Lederer, AKA Ann Landers, were going on the block and when I learned that her desk—the very desk where she sat and wrote her advice column!—was one of them, I got my ass on an airplane. And I got the desk.

While it's highly ironic that the world's smuttiest advice

column will now be written at the same desk where the world's most mainstream (and most popular) advice column was once written, I intended no disrespect in purchasing Ann Landers's desk. I'm not mocking Ann Landers, her column, or her memory—far from it! This is going to make me sound like a huge softy, but the truth is, I bought Landers's desk for sentimental reasons. I started reading her column shortly after I learned to read, and I continued to read it until the end.

A lifelong fan, I bought Ann Landers's desk because I wanted to keep it in the advice business. While the advice I'll be giving from Landers's desk isn't the same advice she would've given . . . that just demonstrates the beautiful thing about advice. According to *The American Heritage Dictionary,* advice is just one person's "opinion about what could or should be done." People who wanted Ann Landers's opinion wrote to her; people who want my opinion write to me. Everybody has opinions, and the only qualification you need in order to give someone advice is being asked for it . . .

In conclusion, I want to emphasize that I am delighted to be the proud, nonironic, no-disrespect-intended owner of Ann Landers's desk. When "Savage Love" is pried from my cold, dead hands, I hope that Ann Landers's desk will be passed on to a fourth- or fifth-generation advice columnist. In the meantime, I hope the ol' gal will peer over my shoulder every once in a while as I work on "Savage Love" at her desk.

Gregory Favre

EDITOR

Sacramento

I t was time to send her a box of her favorite chocolates. Her birthday was coming on July 4. And on three or four occasions each year I contributed to her major vice. She was a self-confessed chocoholic.

But my friend Eppie Lederer died before her birthday. The calendar said she was eighty-three, but that was just a way to mark the years. I don't know if I have ever met anyone with a younger heart and more energy and zest for life than Eppie. And I don't know if I ever met anyone who cared for her work as much as Eppie did, or did it with such care.

From that first column, more than two generations ago, until her last, she put everything she had into making it work and making it serve others as best she could. And that's a lesson for us all.

I had the wonderful opportunity to watch her from two different perspectives: as an editor who bought her column in

256 • Rick Kogan

a number of places and as a managing editor in Chicago who occasionally edited her columns. There are hundreds of editors across the country who received notes or birthday cards from Eppie through the years. And she always started them with, "Dear Boss." Talk about knowing how to manage up, or how to stroke the egos of those who controlled if and where her column would run.

And when it came time to edit her, she was a jewel. The first time, I was a little timid. Well, more than a little. Then the phone rang. "You weren't very tough," the distinctive voice sang out. "I want you to be tough on me."

That was Eppie. She gave advice and she sought it. Most of us are pretty good at the former, not so good at the latter. She knew both were necessary if one is to be truly successful. Now she is gone. No more handwritten notes in the mail. No more boxes of chocolate to send. No more daily doses of her wit and wisdom.

Kathy Mitchell and Marcy Sugar

AUTHORS—"ANNIE'S MAILBOX"

Chicago

KATHY: I moved to Chicago from Indiana in 1969 and was hired on the spot as a typist for Ann Landers. At that time, there were twelve women crammed into a small office like sardines. But we didn't care. We were working hard, trying to keep up with the reader letters—and there were thousands. Eppie had boundless energy and she set the pace. She was a workaholic, but she also loved to laugh—and laugh we did. There was never a dull moment. Two years later, I became one of Eppie's secretaries. I loved it and continued to gain more and more responsibility. I handled public relations; scheduled speeches and media interviews; traveled to events; kept track of her day-to-day life; researched, compiled, and edited booklets; helped locate experts; and became her right arm (as Eppie so kindly put it) and office manager.

MARCY: I was born and raised in Chicago and graduated from the University of Illinois at Chicago in 1973 with a major in mass communications. A friend who was principal of an area secretarial school told me about an opening in Ann Landers's office. I had been a fan of the column for years. He offered to get in touch with her, and Eppie called me at home the same day. She asked me to come to her apartment for an interview that evening. I was surprised to meet her in person; she was so tiny, but what a dynamo! She asked me some personal questions about my upcoming marriage, exactly as if she were my mother, and I was hired immediately. I started with basic research and clerical tasks, and then moved into book-keeping. I also worked with Kathy on Eppie's speaking engagements and helped dig up useful information and opinions to add to the column. In 1979, I left to raise a family, but I came back to work for Eppie shortly after she moved to the *Tribune* in 1987. There I became her editorial assistant, helping to select letters and edit them into column format. If Eppie received a letter that needed an expert opinion, we would get on the phone to research the information and get in touch with the appropriate expert.

KATHY: Even when we traveled, the column came first. Eppie always schlepped hundreds of reader letters along for the ride. She would dictate responses so that she never fell behind. When we finished the mail, it was time to catch up with each other and the events going on in the world. It's fascinating when I think back; it was not uncommon for complete strangers on planes, in airports, on the street, in restaurants, and so on to come up to Eppie and tell her the most intimate details of their lives. Nothing was too sacred. And she never turned anyone away. She was a surrogate mother on the road. If I wasn't in my hotel room when she knocked on the door, she would leave little "love" notes on my pillow to come into her room immediately when I returned. She wanted to know precisely where I went, with whom, the whole nine yards. Not that I was doing anything exciting, but she wanted to know the nitty-gritty. Also, we were never treated like the hired help. If she had a dinner date with a senator, I went along. Wherever she went, I went. It certainly was an education and an opportunity of a lifetime.

MARCY: We really never thought about following in Eppie's footsteps, but things moved very quickly after she died. Her syndicate called and asked if we would be interested in writing the column and after a lot of "should we–shouldn't we," and discussing it with our respective families, we decided to give it our best shot.

KATHY: Actually, we were floored when we were asked. But then we thought we should give it a try. After all, according to her syndicate boss, Rick Newcombe, we were trained by the best and there would be a tremendous void. Her illness was heartbreaking for the "Landers Ladies" as she referred to her staff. Her strength was admirable. Eppie insisted that we not shed tears, but to remember the fact that "she had a wonderful ride and a long life." Her motto was, "Just keep putting one foot in front of the other, Kiddo. We can't let the readers down." But during that time, I was reminded all over again about what a strong person Eppie was and how much she did for people of all walks of life.

MARCY: We thought about all those readers out there, all those people who would miss Eppie's presence. We wanted to continue to help people. We really had no idea how we were going to write the column. It's been quite a learning experience.

There have been times when we don't agree, and if we ever find we can't reach consensus, we will put that in the column. It hasn't happened yet. Kathy and I don't expect to imitate Eppie and we wouldn't try. We will bring our different perspectives to the problems and issues of the day and hope it will show our sense of humor. Eppie had a fabulous sense of humor. But it's so important to give good, sound advice. The most helpful aspect of a newspaper advice column is that it can disseminate useful information to millions of readers at once.

KATHY: There is a tremendous demand for advice and most people want guidance from a nonjudgmental third party, especially if they consider that person someone they can trust. The readers felr that way about Eppie. There will never be another Ann Landers. She was a one-of-a-kind gal. But I really believe that she is looking over our shoulders, helping us along, sort of acting as quiet inspiration. She taught us to be kind, because you never know how much a person may be crying on the inside, but smiling on the outside. Never be judgmental; go with your gut instincts; apologize for mistakes and try to do better next time. Her workaholic disposition obviously rubbed off on us and so did her love for the readers. She made us believe that if you can help just one person a day you have done a good thing.